Sunset

ideas for great
patios & decks

By Scott Atkinson and
the Editors of Sunset Books

Menlo Park, California

Sunset Books

VICE PRESIDENT, GENERAL MANAGER: Richard A. Smeby
VICE PRESIDENT, EDITORIAL DIRECTOR: Bob Doyle
PRODUCTION DIRECTOR: Lory Day
DIRECTOR OF OPERATIONS: Rosann Sutherland
MARKETING MANAGER: Linda Barker
ART DIRECTOR: Vasken Guiragossian
SPECIAL SALES: Brad Moses

Staff for This Book

WRITER: Scott Atkinson
SENIOR EDITOR: Marianne Lipanovich
COPY EDITOR/INDEXER: Barbara J. Braasch
PHOTO DIRECTOR/STYLIST: JoAnn Masaoka Van Atta
ILLUSTRATOR: Bill Oetinger
PRINCIPAL PHOTOGRAPHER: Jaime Hadley
PRODUCTION SPECIALIST: Linda M. Bouchard
PREPRESS COORDINATOR: Danielle Javier
PROOFREADER: Joan Beth Erickson

10 9 8 7 6 5 4 3 2 1
First printing January 2006
Copyright © 2006, Sunset Publishing
Corporation, Menlo Park, CA 94025.
Third edition. All rights reserved, including
the right of reproduction in whole or in
part in any form.

ISBN-13: 978-0-376-01412-2
ISBN-10: 0-376-01412-1
Library of Congress Control
Number: 2005927074
Printed in the United States of America.

For additional copies of *Ideas for Great Patios & Decks* or
any other Sunset book, call 1-800-526-5111 or visit us
at www.sunset.com.

Cover main image: Barbara Jackel Landscape Design;
photography by Marion Brenner.
Top left: David Gibson, The Garden Collection;
photography by Liz Eddison.
Top middle: David Helm; photography by Mark Turner.
Top right: Bernard Trainor Design Associates;
photography by Thomas J. Story.
Cover design by Vasken Guiragossian.

CONTENTS

The Great Outdoors

In the search for more living space, there's one spot we often overlook: outside. What better way to spread out interior traffic, invite the garden in, and frame tranquil views than to build a patio or deck?

This newly revamped entry in Sunset's popular "Ideas for Great…" series is crammed full of ideas and information to help you dream, then design, the outdoor room of your choice. Whether you're looking for a deck, patio, or both, you're sure to find them here.

We would like to thank the many landscaping pros, manufacturers, and homeowners who shared ideas with us or allowed us to photograph their spaces. For the names of professionals whose work is featured here, or for product sources, turn to pages 126–127.

Inside
OUT

FIRST THINGS FIRST: Think of your new patio or deck as an *outdoor room*. Your space might be classically formal or fluid and naturalistic. It could be funky and fun. You may be dreaming of an outdoor kitchen with a pizza oven, a hidden refuge, or a soothing spa. Or maybe you want it all. Interior design ideas are migrating outdoors and new shapes, colors, textures, and amenities abound. Many new designs invite plants to be part of the party. Features like lighting, heaters, arbors, and fountains can also go a long way toward making your outdoor room a reality.

Ready to start brainstorming? You'll find ideas aplenty in the following chapters. Great photos show the latest in landscapes, from tiny gardens of rustic stone to sweeping, multilevel decks in redwood and ipé. A handy shopper's guide gives you a preview of brick, lumber, and man-made decking materials. When you're ready to dig in, take advantage of our solid introduction to patio planning and design.

Ideas and
INSPIRATION

IF YOU'RE LOOKING FOR IDEAS, you've come to the right place. The following pages are bursting with color photos that showcase both patios and decks in action. You'll find scores of materials, formal and informal styles, and landscapes large and small. Feel free to borrow a deck detail here, a patio accent or amenity there. If product availability is a question, take a look at the details in "A Shopper's Guide," beginning on page 80.

A Matter of *Masonry*

PATIO STYLES ARE MADE, at least in part, by the materials you choose for them. For example, nothing says "tradition" like brick. Set in mortar or, more casually, in sand, brick can blend with almost any architectural or landscaping style. Precast concrete pavers can be used in much the same way—in fact, in some areas, "brick-style" pavers are more popular than the real thing.

Poured concrete is perhaps even more adaptable than brick. It can be lightly smoothed or heavily brushed, seeded with colorful pebbles, swirled, stamped, tinted, or molded to resemble another material.

Flat flagstones and stone tiles are ideal for formal paving. For a more informal look, try more irregularly shaped rocks and pebbles, setting them in soil or embedding them in concrete.

From the earthy tones of terra-cotta to the bright primaries of hand-painted accents, ceramic tile can support just about any landscaping style. Just be sure it's slip-resistant.

For economy, good drainage, and a more casual look, consider including loose masonry materials such as pea gravel or decomposed granite in your patio plan.

Left: Colorful, acid-washed concrete sits inside a swirling border of brick and stone.

Opposite page: A formal terrace is floored with 24-inch-square bluestone tiles, which also line the nearby spa.

Far left: Interlocking pavers fit together like puzzle pieces; sand swept into joints makes them stronger.

Left: A blue bench and colorful cushion provide bold contrast to black river rocks tucked between broken concrete pavers.

Above left: Brick dances new steps when laid in a crazy-quilt pattern—a fitting complement to a relaxed setting like this one. A few flat rocks point the way to the garden pond.

Above right: A formal brick backyard is set in classic herringbone and running-bond patterns.

Right: Concrete paver squares join neatly mowed grass to form a firm, but inviting, backyard hardscape.

Opposite page, bottom: How do you make a new tract garden look like it belongs to an old French farmhouse? Try "used" bricks (they're really just tumbled until they look that way).

Below: The formerly bare terrace floor is now a work of art that looks like water swirling over granite. The background is made from colored concrete stamped to mimic stone; blue pool tiles are embedded in the concrete.

Above: This Southwest refuge is all custom-crafted, from the black-bottom spa surrounded by stained concrete coping to the polished granite table with wood-and-metal chairs. A grove of aspens, set in "pools" of river rock, provides four seasons of interest.

Left: A detached patio surrounds a formal water garden. The concrete pavers are rigidly rectangular, but softened by abundant border plantings.

Right: This intricate stone mosaic is seeded in mortar like raisins in pudding.

Far right: Concrete-and-wood steps lead down to two circular landing pads made from tightly fitted cobblestones.

Right top: Formal bluestone tiles make a cool counterpart to some flaming fall color.

Right bottom: Puffs of green baby's tears soften bands of African slate. Seeded-aggregate concrete flanks the "path."

Below: Sandstone slabs team up with river rocks and adobe walls. Enclosing walls and a decorative window give this patio the feel of a sheltered, but open, outdoor room.

Left: Bright blue ceramic tiles sprinkled amid bricks set up this garden's blue-and-terra-cotta color scheme, which is echoed by the hand-thrown ceramic pot and in the flowers' hues.

Opposite page: Slick ceramic can be trouble outdoors, but some new floor tiles are toothy enough for safe footing. And while they resemble both stone and terra-cotta, these porcelain pavers are easier to maintain.

Below: Square French pavers floor a formal front courtyard that also includes a classic tiled fountain.

Below: Most designers try to tame the landscape, but the residents of this property chose instead to restore the native habitat. Informal clearings of decomposed granite circulate throughout the plantings and connect the buildings.

Opposite page, top: Color, inspired by Indian saris, vaults this classically simple arrangement of walls, trees, fire pit, and neutral gravel floor into the twenty-first century.

Opposite page, bottom: This 10- by 10-foot "blue room" features a celestial-patterned mosaic. The designer used ceramic tile remnants, laid in adhesive atop plastic netting. After, the space between tiles was filled with decomposed granite.

The Warmth
of Wood

WOOD'S WARM COLOR AND SOFT TEXTURE bring something of the forest into your landscape, and if stained, it can hold its own in even the most formal company. A deck provides a durable surface requiring little or no grading and a minimum of maintenance. Because decking is raised above the ground and can dry quickly, it's a natural wherever drainage is a problem.

Softwoods like redwood and cedar are traditional, but hardwood imports offer new options. For even less maintenance and a lower environmental impact, consider so-called composite decking that's made from recycled materials. Note, however, that you'll still need wood or another material for structural members—composites aren't rated for strength.

Typically, any deck more than 30 inches above ground requires a railing or similar barrier. Beyond safety, railings contribute an important design element, too. What's the view? Use railings to frame it or block it. Fill gaps with vertical slats, safety glass, acrylic, or metal grillwork.

Left: It's wood—no, it's plastic. The composite decking is joined by white-painted wood railings.

Opposite page: A clear cedar deck can take all the moisture that Washington skies can deliver; its curved lines echo the shape of the koi pond just below. "Boulders" rimming the pond are made of concrete, sculpted by hand and spattered with latex paint to mimic the color and texture of native stone.

Above: A progression of small pocket decks ties three outdoor areas together and offers options for enjoying a leisurely lifestyle.

Right: One small step up from the stone-rimmed spa, this compact, low-level deck still provides plenty of room for relaxing.

Opposite page: This low entry deck bridges house and landscape while providing a smooth surface and efficient drainage. Leisurely curves lead the eye toward the front archway beyond.

Top: A soothing hot tub holds center stage on this private garden platform. Note the crafted patterns and accents on the deck surface.

Above: A private spa alcove is wrapped in the same wood and styling as the main deck nearby.

Left: This split-level hardwood deck floats among a forest of twisted oaks; baked enamel railing inserts preserve the view.

Opposite page: This broad backyard structure is at home with the surrounding forest, but its decking "boards" aren't wood—they're splinter-free composite made largely from recycled plastic. Built-in wooden bench seating surrounds a fire pit that, when covered, becomes a coffee table.

Right: Patios and decks aren't mutually exclusive. Here, slate and hardwood decking both share a "floating" substructure, allowing different looks on different levels.

Above: Staining can spruce up dull decking wood and match deck to house, or—in this case—the green garden beyond.

Right: The circular pocket deck within brick headers is built from composite decking made of recycled wood and virgin polymers.

Below: Finely-crafted curved railings are mirrored by built-in benches on this spacious elevated deck.

Opposite page, top left: A wraparound deck— or *engawa*—links rooms all along the house. Sliding shoji panels allow the breezeway to be battened down in bad weather.

Opposite page, top right: A low-level deck was shaped with lively curves and squiggles. This organic alternative melds deck to garden.

Right, top: Armed with a jig saw, the owner of this deck gave each 1¼- by 4-inch cedar rail a whimsical shape.

Right, bottom: Railings that offer good protection can block a desirable view, but not when they're "windows" made of tempered glass or acrylic.

Far right: It's the details that count. Here, railings are joined by built-in benches and a corner planter box.

Enter the
Outdoor Room

MORE AND MORE OF US are relaxing the line between indoors and outdoors, creating a leisurely transition between the two. The effect begins with your choice of patio doors. French and sliding models are time-honored options, but consider other types, too. You can also group glazed doors with window units to make a window wall that seems to merge directly with the landscape.

Use verticals—fences, walls, trellises, and screens—to define the room and add privacy. A shady arbor or plant-lined pergola forms the roof. In harsh climates, the sunroom is an option as an indoor-outdoor space. Some sunrooms can be opened up when the sun shines and battened down when hard winds blow. If you're planning a new home or an extensive remodel, you may wish to incorporate an interior courtyard, or atrium, into your plans. And don't rule out the classic porch, currently enjoying a comeback.

Furnishings and accents with indoor heritage set the tone. Add container plants, a rug, comfy pillows, artwork, and lighting. And don't forget other amenities like a heater, fire pit, or fireplace. For ideas, see pages 50–55.

Left: Climbing roses clothe an 8-foot-tall steel frame, creating an open but enclosed outdoor space for reading and relaxation.

Opposite page: This outdoor room forms an architectural extension of the house, and includes an arbor, curtains, and a stone-lined stream that runs below the concrete floor.

Left: Limestone tiles floor a dazzling outdoor room, featuring kitchen and barbecue, stylish arbor, and eave-mounted patio heater.

Top: A rustic desert ramada has posts and cross-beams of mesquite plus a roof of ocotillo canes. A living ocotillo screen beyond blocks out an unwanted view.

Above: Lunch is served in a secluded corner of this leafy patio. An attractive retaining wall was built into a hillside to form the space; recycled timbers were used for the overhead. A wall fountain and antique corbels add touches of romance and Old World charm.

Above: Talk about an outdoor room: this deckside gazebo makes a private sleeping retreat, complete with its own lighting and redwood trees.

Right: Colorful fabrics give this outdoor room drama—especially when lit from within. Saris make the walls; canvas panels form the roof.

Above, left: A classic sunroom, or solarium, brings in plenty of sun while barring bugs and breezes. The masonry floor helps store heat.

Above, right: Finished wood decking, heavy mesh screens, and translucent ceiling panels are durable elements that seamlessly blend this comfortable sun porch with its surroundings.

Right: The owner wanted a solarium, but the house's roofline didn't permit it. Instead, they upgraded their existing deck with a freestanding gazebo: a simple gabled roof with skylights rests on four Doric columns that replicate the ones in their living room.

Opposite page: To add a sense of enclosure to the deck, the owners created a "floating wall" along one side by hanging framed windows from galvanized steel chains anchored to the overhead beams with eye bolts. 'Concord' grape and morning glory vines ramble over the trellis roof, shading the deck in summer, dangling clusters of ripe fruit in August, then—when leafless in winter—allowing sunlight through.

Remote
Retreats

GETTING AWAY FROM IT ALL gets tougher and tougher, but a detached patio or deck can offer restful privacy while utilizing an otherwise empty garden space. Your retreat can be tiny. A small paved clearing, borrowed from the garden, might contain just enough solid brick or flagstone to anchor a bench or chairs, drinks, and a fat novel or two.

Or it can be more substantial. A freestanding deck or a bower (a rustic shelter with arbor roof, built-in bench, and perhaps a trickling fountain) might frame a distant view or face inward to a quiet reflecting pond.

Gazebos form classic retreats. Evocative of country bandstands on summer evenings, they become poetic-looking accents and romantic garden destinations. If you're space-challenged, look elsewhere, towards a side-yard pocket-deck, an enclosed front courtyard, a reclaimed driveway, or up on the roof.

Remote retreats take beautifully to amenities: decorative light fixtures, hammocks or swings, fountains or spas. Make the route to your hide-away direct or circuitous; mark the spot with a clearly visible overhead structure; or use subtle screening and tall plants as camouflage.

Left: A casual flagstone path detours around a water-filled basin en route to the lushly planted terrace.

Opposite page: This secluded teahouse sits atop a low-level deck that rests on sturdy boulders amidst lush plantings, waterfalls, and a pond that's home to flickering orange koi.

Right: Blue chairs and a white-painted arbor are tinged with yellow sunrise light. The owner-built structure, floored with flagstones and soft blue star creeper, sits atop a hillside garden and makes a great vantage point for morning or evening views.

Below: Tucked into a tousled array of flowers and grasses, a bentwood chair offers a quiet retreat at the end of a trail of stepping-stones.

Right: This 6- by 13-foot sleeping pavilion occupies a wooden platform near a small pond. Gauzy curtains frame the entrance and provide privacy and bug protection when needed. A shallow gabled roof covered with translucent fiberglass shelters the area from rain and drizzle without blocking light.

Above: A "repurposed" bathtub is the centerpiece for a new outdoor soaking oasis. Hot and cold running water fills a newly enameled green tub set on a thick stone slab. Surrounding the slab is a flagstone patio with Japanese black pebbles in the cracks. Screens made from bamboo and birch branches add privacy.

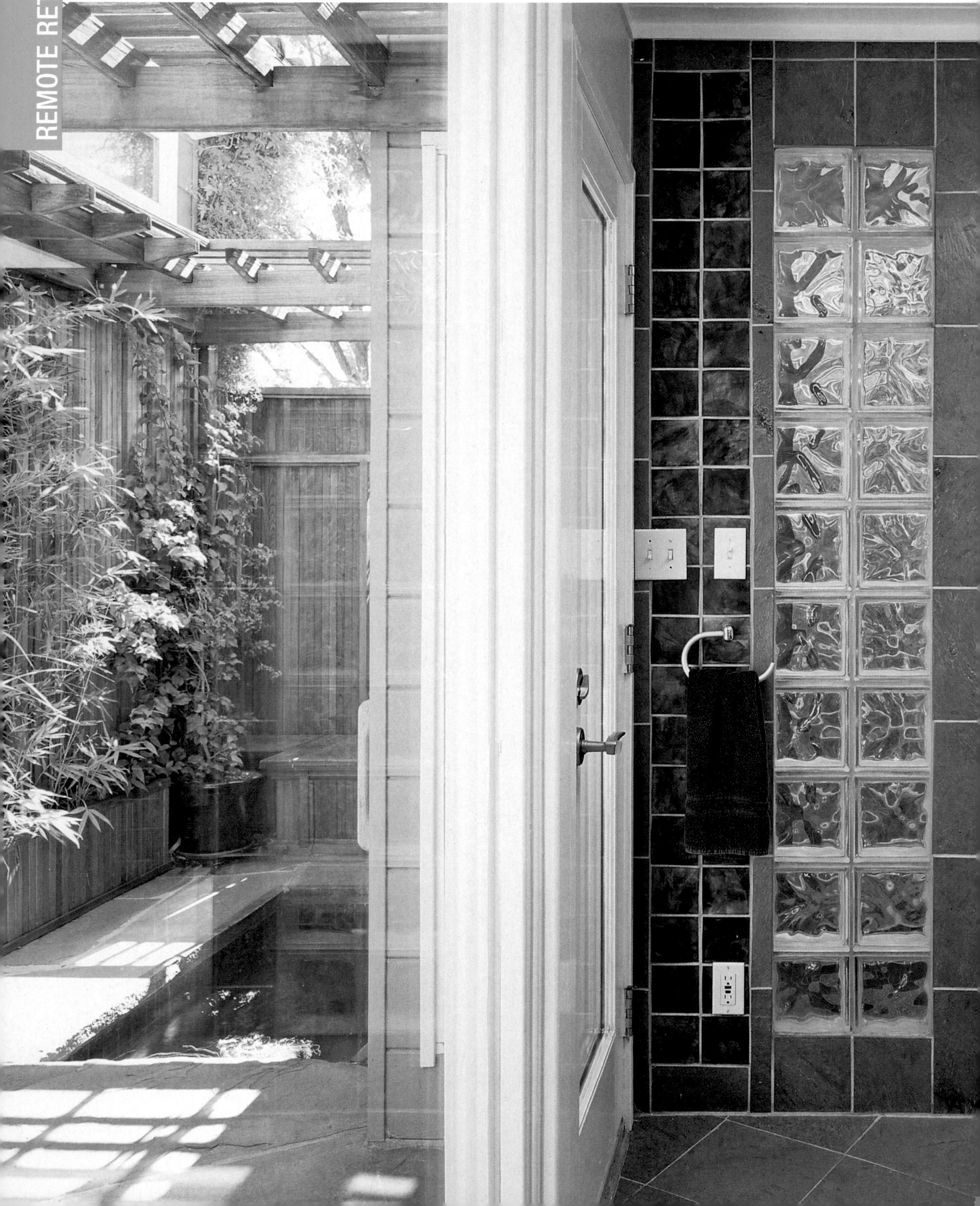

Above: Multiple stacked decks save space and serve multiple functions. The "public" deck is up top, a private bedroom deck below.

Right: Up on the roof, concrete pavers float in a river-rock "stream" that ends in a private sitting area.

Left: Inside meets outside in this owner-built, master-suite bath featuring a French door that opens to the nearby private patio and an in-ground spa pool.

Small-Space *Solutions*

WHEN SPACE IS SHORT, your landscape should work harder. Vertical stacking is one way to go. You can also intensify the space by creating small, separate areas. Pay particular attention to your use of paving; because the space is small, it must stand up to close scrutiny. A set of glazed doors or a window wall can link house and garden, stretching space in both directions.

Small-space designs often employ a deliberate sense of "misdirection." Use winding paths, grouped containers, screens, arbors, and plantings to slow traffic, to frame tiny views, and to create hidden spots that blur boundaries. Even a tiny pond or pool can make a space seem larger by creating an illusion of depth and by reflecting the sky and surrounding surfaces.

To protect privacy, grow a screen of green. Tall plants or vine-covered arbors block out views. A trickling waterfall or fountain masks noise. Soft low-voltage light fixtures or some festive rope lights can make even the smallest space special.

Left: As the owner-builder of this backyard tea garden says, "It's all about enclosure." The compact retreat was made special with a peaceful teahouse and pond.

Opposite page: Low-level decking and Saltillo tiles beyond are angled to enhance a small space. A trickling wall fountain makes a tranquil focal point off the living room. Tall plantings and an arbor offer a sense of enclosure and screen off the neighbors' house.

Left: This urban garden looks larger, thanks to the designers' division of space. On the lower level, a small patio offers seating for intimate gatherings. Three steps up, an open brick courtyard accommodates larger groups. The rose-covered arbor and upward-arching gate create a circle that frames attractive views.

Left: This narrow side-yard space includes clumping bamboo, a shallow pond with river-rock edging, Japanese maples, low-growing mondo grass, and stepping pads of black canterra tiles.

Above: A set of new French doors open on a once-ignored side yard and a striking fountain. The buff-colored concrete path has inset terra-cotta tiles and matching diamond-shaped borders.

Left: Challenged for space? Look up front. Here, the arching branches of a Japanese snowdrop tree frame an inviting entry deck.

Above: Three rooms look out onto the narrow backyard shown here; they each now have a fine view. Water streams from wall-mounted spouts into a narrow dipping pool, which is lined with terra-cotta above, and a dense, waterproof limestone below the waterline.

Left: How do you squeeze a lap pool into a modest backyard? Try placing it, like this one, on the diagonal. The pool is 35 feet long and 8 feet wide, with a small spa on one side.

Opposite page: A cramped, steep lot posed a challenge, but this multilevel, multiuse structure shows a creative response. Sitting areas top retaining walls; luxurious plantings and earthy paving materials soften hard lines.

That's *Entertainment*

WHILE FAMILY COOKOUTS are traditionally centered around the barbecue, you can go a step further—and bring the comfort and convenience of an indoor kitchen to poolside or patio. Commercial cooktops abound. Custom units may incorporate built-in smokers, woks, or pizza ovens as well.

Supporting players include prepping and serving areas, storage cabinets, a vent hood, an under-counter refrigerator, a sink with disposer, a dishwasher, a wet bar, and a dining area.

Most outdoor entertainment centers are at least partially sheltered overhead. Depending on the site's exposure and microclimate, you may need to add screens, trellises, or even heavy bi-fold or sliding doors to help screen wind and hot sun or provide temporary enclosure during winter months.

Speaking of weather, plan for some heat if you're entertaining in the off season. Portable heaters and fire pits are easy options—or go all out with built-in benches and fire pit, or a full-scale fireplace.

Left: A desert gathering spot includes built-in stone benches and a matching fire pit.

Opposite page: This Tuscan-inspired outdoor kitchen is a casual yet elegant environment for dining—the owners even have Thanksgiving dinner here.

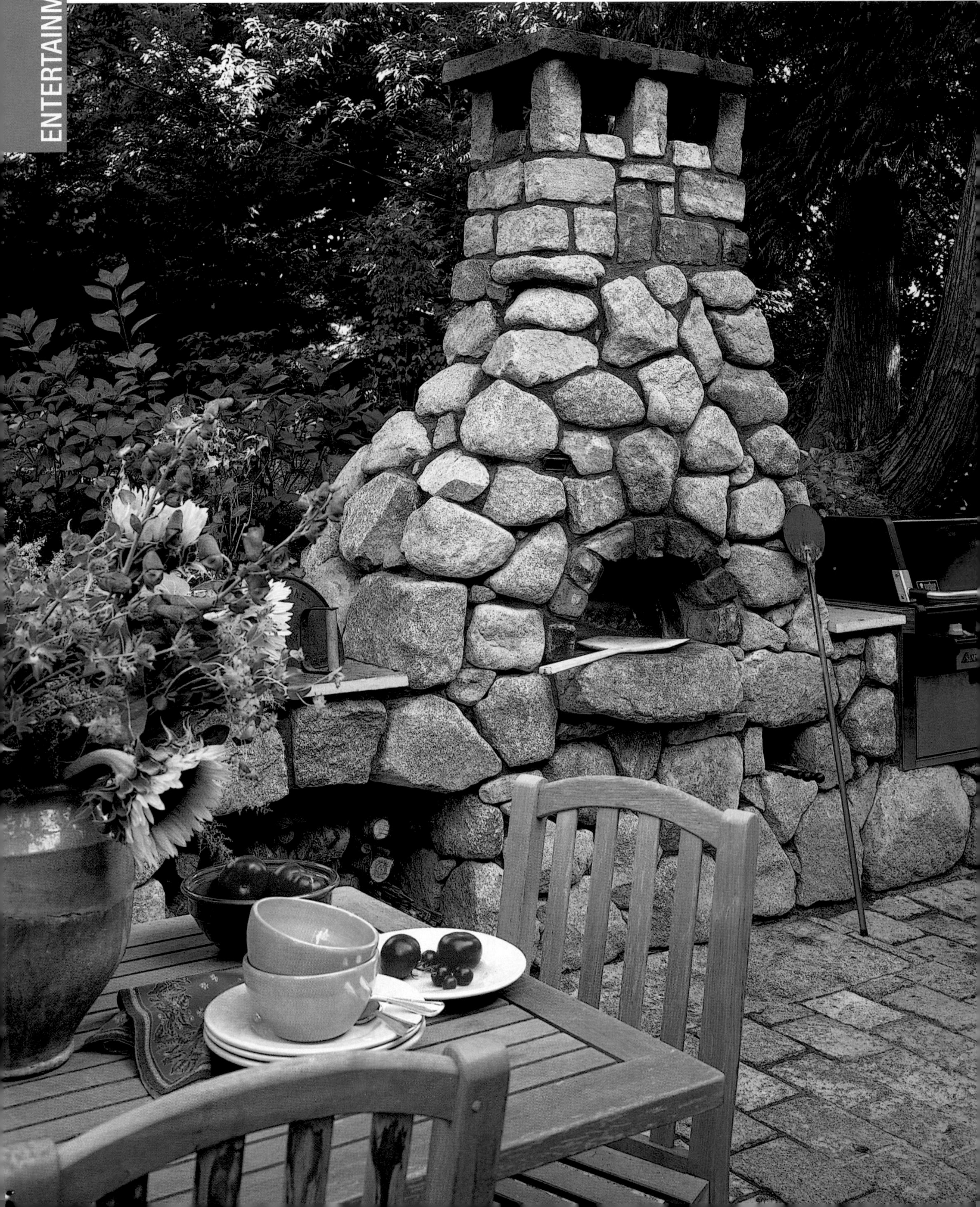

Above and right: A granite-tiled eating counter backs a curved entertaining area that's fully integrated into a poolside patio design. The well-equipped kitchen is set two steps below general patio level, making serving and conversing more comfortable. The lowered floor also encourages swimmers to join in, using the tile-topped "tables" along the pool's edge.

Opposite page: This wood-fired outdoor oven sees plenty of pizza-baking and chicken-roasting action. The carefully crafted granite structure houses a prefabricated oven insert, a chimney, a wood bin, and even a digital timer.

Opposite page: A cheery chiminea burns away in one corner of the fitted flagstone terrace, protected by spark arrester and screen.

Left: In this minimalist hardscape, a simple fire pit in a stone bowl adds evening drama to a poolside area—a study in cool azure and shades of green.

Below: With its handsome fireplace and flanking storage niches, this covered patio makes a cozy outdoor room.

Just Add *Water*

WHETHER TRICKLING AS A WALL FOUNTAIN, meandering as a stream, or collected as a full-scale garden pond stuffed with lilies and fish, a decorative water feature brings tranquility to any outdoor environment. Your pond may be formal or informal. It needn't be built in; even the tiniest layout can hold a tub garden or a small spill fountain.

The surround sets the mood: with the addition of boulders, flagstones, bridges, and other freeform edgings, naturalistic pools and spas can double as garden ponds. Nonslip masonry is safest, but wood stays cooler underfoot.

Spas come in a rainbow of colors, shapes, and textures; materials range from sleek acrylic to formal concrete. Go informal with a wooden hot tub, or opt for a recycled bathtub or steel watering trough. Be sure to plan shelter from wind, rain, and the neighbors.

In recent years many swimming pools have been slimmed to fit home landscapes rather than overpower them. Some can be shoehorned into tight sites and integrated more easily into relatively modest schemes. The lap pool is a case in point.

Left: How do you landscape a steep hillside? A three-tiered waterfall proved right for this site. The homeowner designed the falls, then left the construction to a professional.

Opposite page: Why wait 'til vacation to escape to Kauai or Bali? Here, tropical plants edge the lagoonlike pool, which has a shallow bench and a waterfall.

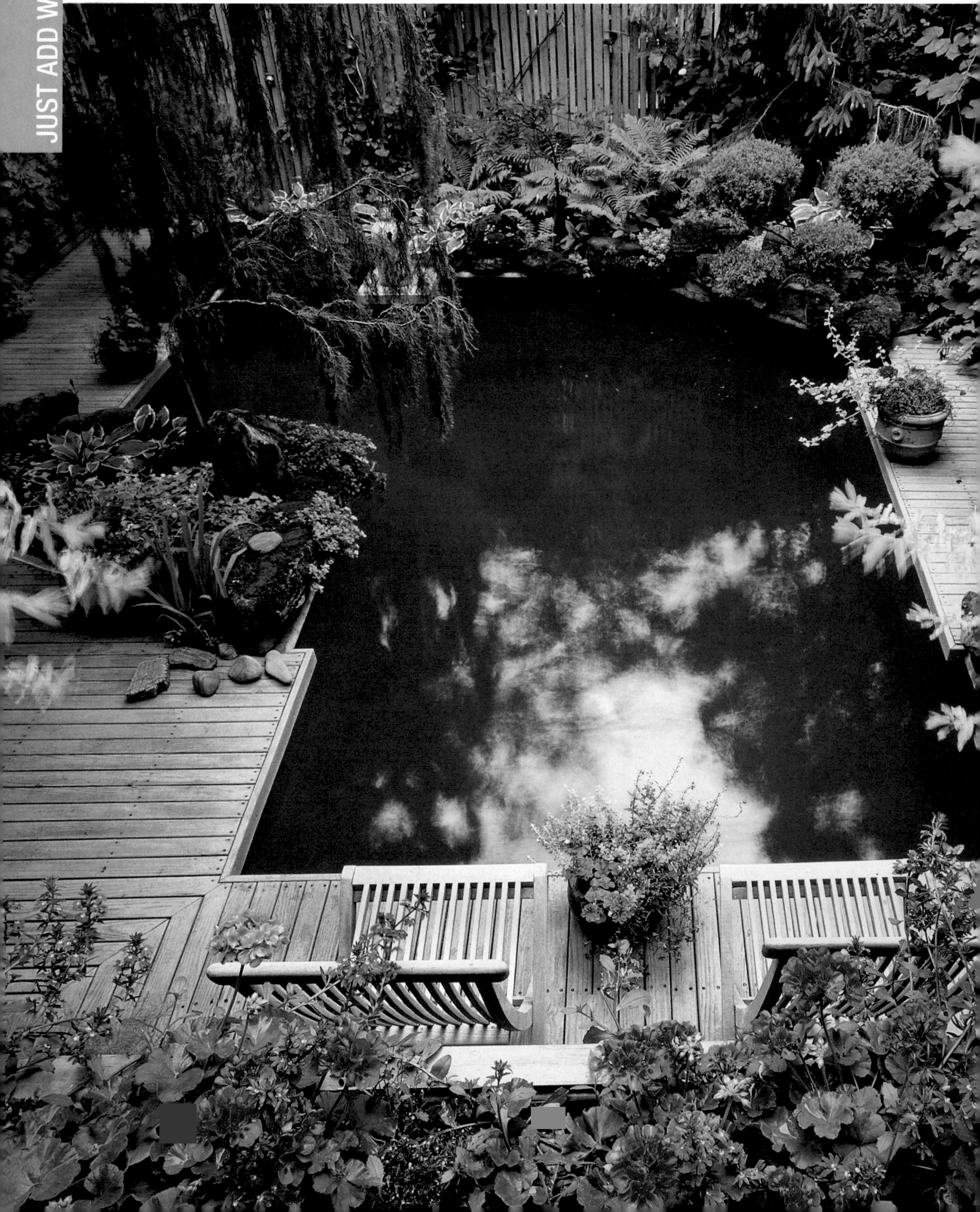

Top: A flagstone-rimmed, "vanishing-edge" pool is seemingly cantilevered beyond the canyon rim—the secret is a retaining wall hidden from sight, plus a recirculating pump.

Above: This small soaking pool is fed by a water channel recessed in the top of a curved retaining wall, which also wraps around the spacious seating area above.

Left: A concrete pool goes organic with overhanging wood decking, boulders, and border plantings.

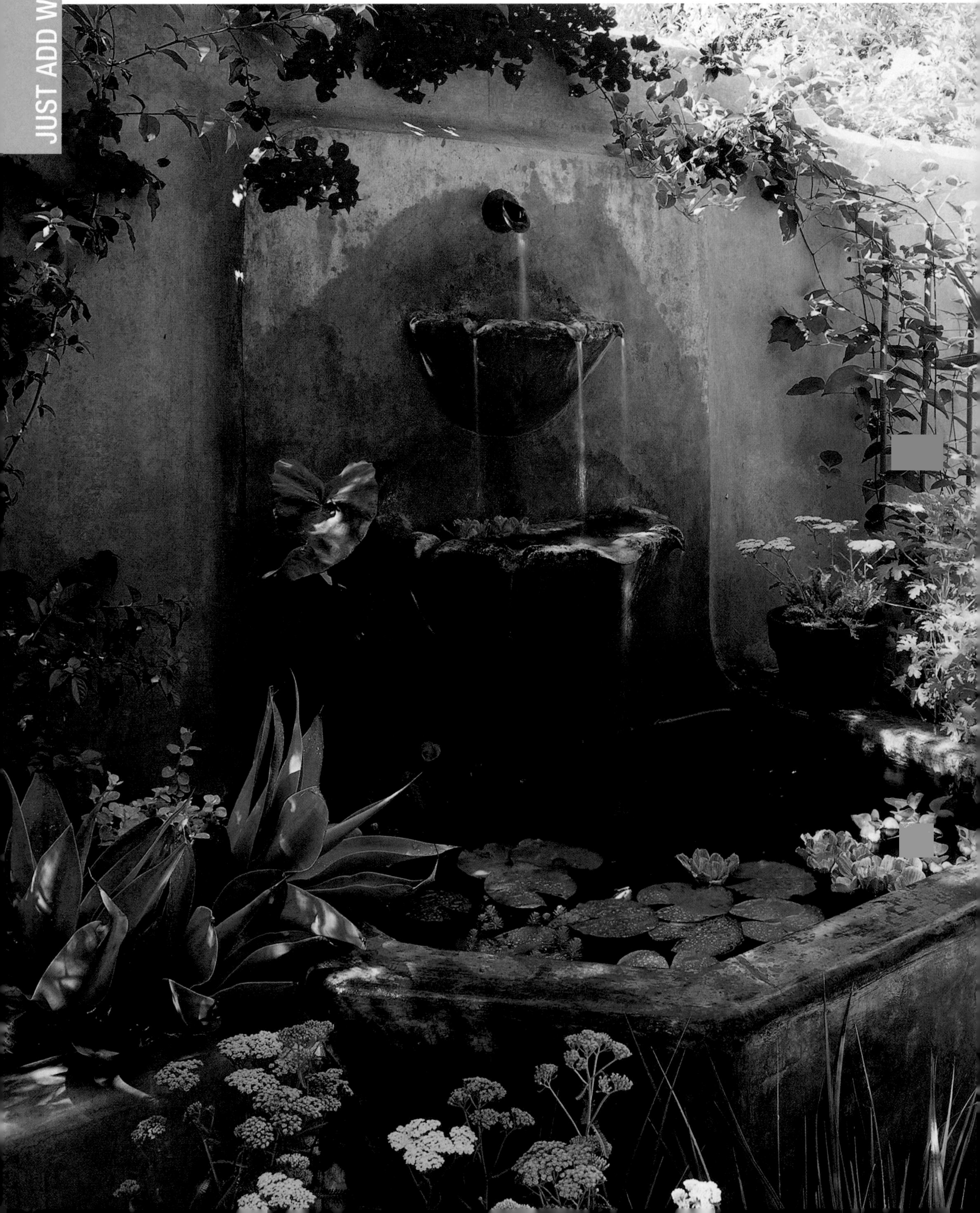

Opposite page: Against a rustic stucco wall, water spills out of scalloped bowls amidst blazing bougainvillea. Even a tranquil trickle can help mask neighborhood noise.

Right: A vivid purple bench overlooks a poured-concrete pond with a hot fuchsia rim. Projecting from the pond, black concrete columns are topped by pots of splashy plants. Hidden PVC pipes carry water up through the columns, turning them into trickle fountains.

Above: In this bird's-eye view, a burbling bubble fountain forms a focal point for the flagstone "living room."

Right: A rustic wooden deck steps down past the matching tub garden, formed from a half barrel.

A Place
for Plants

WE'VE NOTED THE RISE IN OUTDOOR ROOMS, where indoors meets outdoors. But there's also a trend towards blurring the boundaries between patio and garden. Any patio or deck hardscape can be softened with greenery. Portable containers transport annuals and perennials, shrubs, and vegetables to favorable locations.

On the other hand, built-in planting spaces lend a custom look to your structure. Add formal masonry beds or leave planting pockets between paving units. Incorporate planters into steps or level changes, deck railings, or built-in benches.

Or go vertical. Trellises make great plant supports and double as privacy screens. Arbors launch the theme overhead, adding welcome shade in season. Why not add a patioside potting shed or greenhouse?

Don't forget to water! Drip systems and minisprinklers are most efficient, especially when teamed with timers and/or moisture sensors. Snake drip tubing up arbors and through paving joints. If you wish to water the old-fashioned way, be sure there's an accessible hose bibb nearby.

Left: Wire baskets hang from the deck railing, adding extra real estate for some scarlet geraniums.

Opposite page: Foliage forms this private niche for couch and table. The grape arbor is joined by lush border plantings and a collection of containers.

Above: Going vertical? Trellises and hanging baskets aren't the only options. A simple stepladder can hold pots, too—with no hardware required.

Below: Besides fending off hungry deer and elk, this Idaho garden's sandstone walls also retain solar heat that radiates into the garden. Pots of roses and lavender surround the patio; creeping thyme fills cracks between flagstones.

Above: Want a solution for boring patio walls? This twiggy trellis has horizontal grids built from birch branches fastened to spacers screwed into the house wall. The arching tops are formed by bundles of twigs bound with copper wire.

Opposite page: Heavy wisteria vines are supported by an arching iron arbor accented by precast concrete columns. The foliage forms a shady canopy for outdoor dining.

Opposite page: This garden designer paints with plants and accessories to play up color contrasts. The jaunty greenhouse also helps link patio and garden.

Right: Raised beds meet patio. Framed with untreated redwood, the beds are lined on the bottom with landscape fabric and along the sides with polyethylene film to keep moisture from contacting the wood. A drip-irrigation system waters the plants.

Above: The owner turned galvanized livestock-watering tanks into raised beds. In the bottom of each tank, he drilled several 1-inch drain holes and covered them with screen to prevent the soil from draining out.

Right: This balcony was just a narrow landing outside a condominium's back door until the resident turned it into a bright and lively landscape of flowers. Most of the railing now disappears in a sweep of blooms in window boxes.

Lighting *It Up*

SAFETY, SECURITY, AND STYLE can all be served with a good outdoor lighting scheme. The only restriction is to keep both glare and wattage at a low level. To stop glare, place fixtures either very low (as along a walk) or very high. Use several softer lights strategically placed around the patio and yard rather than one harsh bulb.

You can choose a standard 120-volt system or use a low-voltage scheme. For additional fixture details, see pages 98–99.

On decks and patios, low light levels are usually enough for quiet conversation or alfresco dining. Maybe candles or lanterns are all you need. Add stronger lights for serving or barbecuing areas. Decorative minilights help outline trees and lend sparkle to your landscape. Festive rope lights are also useful for marking steps, railings, and walkways.

Don't forget the view from inside. To avoid a "black hole" effect, try to balance light levels on both sides of a picture window or French doors. Add depth with medium-strength light in the foreground, soften the middle ground, and save the high wattage for background.

Left: Splayed candle lanterns tilt casually to and fro along a winding garden path.

Opposite page: Subtle night lighting highlights plantings and helps turn an arbor-topped patio into an around-the-clock extension of interior space.

Right: This octagonal umbrella casts cooling shade by day and warm light by night. Four bulbs nestle at the top of the center pole, bouncing a soft glow off the umbrella and back to the table.

Below: This garden glows when the sun goes down. Effects include dramatic uplighting below trees, downlighting to brighten the patio, ground-level lighting to highlight planting beds, backlighting behind the potted trees, and wall washing on the end wall and fireplace.

Top: What appears to be an underwater meteor shower (or maybe millions of aquatic lightning bugs) is actually more than 2,000 fiber-optic lights.

Above: Recessed, sealed well lights graze colorful concrete walls, forming a soft, textured backdrop for alfresco dining. Candles atop the table add their warm, decorative glow.

Below left: Chunky candles on decorative holders wash this plastered wall niche with a warm golden glow.

Below right: Blown-glass oil lamps on spiral stakes add a soft, tropical touch on a festive summer night.

Left: These translucent glass blocks glow from below to accent both nearby plantings and the patio itself.

Above: Loops of wire suspend candles in antique carriage lamps and lidless mason jars, which the owner calls "light pendants," from the overhead lath.

Left: Tiny, low-voltage lights are tucked behind a deck overhang, safely lighting a short step.

Finishing *Touches*

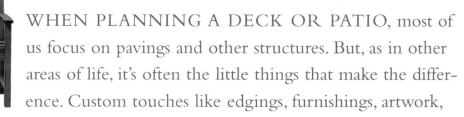

WHEN PLANNING A DECK OR PATIO, most of us focus on pavings and other structures. But, as in other areas of life, it's often the little things that make the difference. Custom touches like edgings, furnishings, artwork, storage spots, and even hose bibbs or power outlets can go a long way towards turning a hardscape into a comfortable outdoor room.

Something as simple as rounding over decking edges or railings can convert your outdoor room from a "boat dock" to a piece of furniture. Speaking of furnishings, opt for freestanding patio furniture or built-ins, or both (see pages 96–97). Build benches into wide steps or transitions between levels. For fun, add overhead support for a porch swing or hammock. Pillows and throw rugs add portable style and comfort without a lot of work.

Think creature comforts. What about a portable propane heater or folksy wood-burning chiminea? Or, on the flip side, how about a set of spray misters for scorching summer days? Patio umbrellas are a tried-and-true weather buffer. A built-in, barside TV and/or weatherproof audio speakers are just some of the other options.

Left: So your outdoor room lacks a view? Paint one in, like this trompe l'oeil "window" recess.

Opposite page: Whether it hangs from the sheltered confines of a front porch or off the branch of a backyard tree, a swaying swing is sure to transport you away from the hurried pace of your workday.

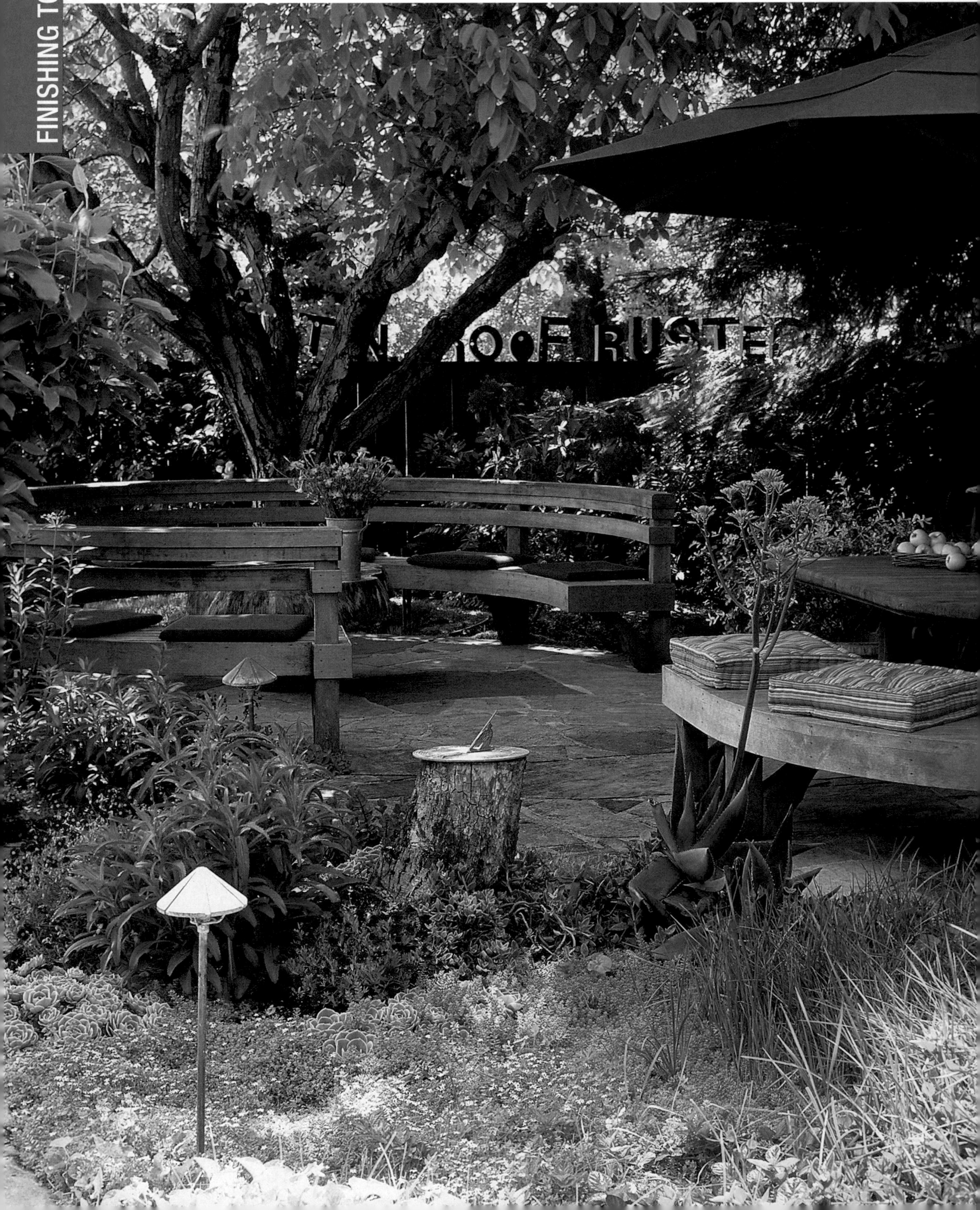

Opposite page: Curved, built-in benches abound in this outdoor entertaining alcove.

Right: Here's the ultimate built-in: an outdoor couch growing out of an adobe and stucco retaining wall. Puffy cushions and a soft seat ensure a comfortable visit; when weather threatens, just tote them inside.

Above: A one-of-a-kind table was built from a recycled iron gate nested in a new frame and topped with sturdy glass.

Right: Most arbors carry vines, but this two-post design holds up a hammock, too. Be sure to set posts securely in concrete.

Below: Painted lattice, painted table and chairs, and painted artwork enliven this outdoor room.

Right: This pocket-size patio garden is an homage to Central America. Junglelike plants complement the leafy cushion fabric. Collectibles are reminders of pre-Columbian culture and Spanish mission influence.

Left: Spray misters team with overhead lattice to create a cool patio oasis in an otherwise hot climate. In fact, this outdoor room even supports a lush growth of ferns.

Far left: Along the patio border, a sandbox provides a welcome alternative to nearby adult activities.

Left: A coiled hose is a necessary evil in a garden—you need one, but who wants to see it? Instead, you can store one or two hoses inside the lid of a handsome bench. The hinged top is held open with a hook and eye.

A *Shopper's* GUIDE

WHETHER YOU'RE LEANING towards wood or concrete, this chapter can help you sort out your options. Here we'll try to demystify some of the ritual and jargon surrounding lumberyards and home centers. Local information can also be a big help, too, so ask your building department or garden supplier about the best deck stain, tile sealer, or base treatment for use in your area. Need more detailed planning info? Take a look at Chapter Three, "How To Do It."

bricks & pavers

Leaning towards tradition? Brick dates back at least 6,000 years. To make bricks, clay is mixed with water, then hand–molded or machine-extruded, and fired in a kiln. A rich palette of colors and a broad range of styles make brick a perennial favorite for garden paving. Want more options? Consider concrete pavers, the modern alternative to brick.

Brick types

Of the bewildering variety of bricks available, only two basic kinds are used for garden construction: tough-textured common brick and smoother-surfaced face brick.

Most garden paving is done with common brick. People like its familiar warm color and texture, and it's less expensive than face brick. Common brick is more porous than face brick and less uniform in color and size (common bricks may vary up to ¼ inch in length).

More often used for facing buildings than for paving, face brick is best reserved for elegant raised beds, attractive edgings, and other areas where its smoothness won't present a safety hazard.

In addition to the familiar orange-red, some manufacturers offer bricks in colors created by the addition of chemicals to the clay. Manganese can give a metallic blue tone. Iron produces a dark speckling. "Flashed" brick is fired unevenly to darken either its face or edge.

Used brick has uneven surfaces and streaks of old mortar that can look very attractive in an informal setting. Manufactured "used" or "rustic" bricks cost about the same as the genuine article and are easier to find. Firebricks, blond-colored

Left: Curved, mortared edgings outline a striking brick-in-sand patio, formed from new "used" bricks.

A BRICK SAMPLER

and porous, provide attractive accents but don't wear well as general paving.

The typical brick is about 8 by 4 by 2⅜ inches thick. "Paver" bricks, which are made to use atop a concrete base, are roughly half the thickness of standard bricks. "True" (or "mortarless") pavers are a uniform 4 by 8 inches (plus or minus ⅛ inch) and can be invaluable for laying a complex pattern with tightly butted joints.

Paver possibilities

Concrete pavers are no longer limited to the ubiquitous 12-inch squares you've seen for years. Paver shapes now include circles, rectangles, triangles, rough cobblestones, and contours that interlock. Easily installed atop a packed sand bed (see page 119), pavers are an ideal choice for do-it-yourselfers. Large pavers can also be spaced apart and surrounded with grass, a ground cover, or gravel for textural interest.

Interlocking pavers fit together like puzzle pieces.

When laid in sand with closed (butted) joints, they form a surface even more rigid than brick. Some interlocking shapes are proprietary, available only at a few outlets or from distributors.

Concrete "bricks," available in classic red as well as imitation used or antique styles, are increasingly popular as substitutes for the real thing, and in many areas cost significantly less.

Some professionals cast their own pavers in custom shapes, textures, and colors—mimicking adobe, stone, or tile, for example.

INTERLOCKING PAVERS

CONCRETE PAVERS

CUSTOM-MADE PAVERS

CONCRETE "BRICKS"

concrete

Though once dismissed as cold and forbidding, poured concrete is sporting new looks. Used with the proper forms and reinforcement, concrete can conform to almost any shape. And if you get tired of the concrete surface later on, you can use it as a foundation for a new pavement of brick, stone, or tile set in mortar.

Below: Classic concrete finishes include (1) semismooth; (2) broomed; (3) salt-finished; (4) exposed aggregate; (5) travertine; and (6) stamped.

Shopping for concrete

Strictly speaking, concrete is a mixture of portland cement, sand, aggregate, and water. Cement is what binds everything together and gives the finished product its hardness. The sand and aggregate (usually gravel) act as fillers and control shrinkage.

Buying bagged, dry concrete is expensive but convenient, at least for small jobs. The standard 90-pound bag makes ⅔ cubic foot of concrete, enough to cover about a 16-inch-square area 4 inches deep.

For bigger projects, it pays to order portland cement, sand, and aggregate in bulk and mix them with a power mixer. Some dealers also supply trailers containing about 1 cubic yard of wet, ready-mixed concrete (about enough for an 8- by 10-foot patio). For larger-scale work, a commercial transit-mix truck can deliver enough concrete to fill large patio forms in a single pour.

Exact formulas of concrete vary from area to area, depending on local climate, season, and materials. Be sure to ask your supplier about the best formula for your needs.

Jazzing it up

You can wash or sandblast concrete to uncover the aggregate. Or embed colorful pebbles and stones in it—a finish known as seeded aggregate. The addition of larger river rocks and fieldstones can also give new interest to a dull slab.

Other ways to modify standard concrete surfaces include brooming, color-dusting, staining, masking, sandblasting, acid-washing, and salt-finishing. A professional can also stamp and tint concrete to resemble stone, tile, or brick. Stamped "joints" can then be grouted to look like unit masonry.

Concrete makeovers

If you have a deteriorating concrete patio, you can either demolish it and build anew or give it a face-lift.

Professionally applied solutions include the treatment of concrete

Right: A blue concrete river meanders through a sideyard patio, past fragmented islands in a gray field.

with one of three methods: bonding, staining, or top-coating.

In bonding, a mixture of colored cement and a binder is sprayed over the entire surface. Then a design is created by the use of incised patterns or imitation grout lines.

Several companies offer chemical stains in a variety of colors that can be applied directly to the surface of an existing slab to give it a camouflaging patina.

One innovative top coat is made of ground-up bits of colored recycled rubber bonded together with a clear epoxy. Or you can cover the concrete with seeded aggregate. Or float on a new colored mix, which can then be stamped or textured.

CONCRETE COMPONENTS

Left: The sun's rays were created with black and tan acid stains. Nearby paving received a brown stain.

stone

Stone pavings have the appeal of a thoroughly natural material, and most are very durable. Flat flagstones and cut stone tiles are both great for patios. For a more rustic look, try mixing in some irregularly shaped rocks and pebbles.

Flagstone

Technically, flagstone is any flat stone that's either naturally thin or split from rock that cleaves easily. The selection pictured below gives you an idea of the range of colors and textures available at masonry and building supply yards. Cost depends on where you live in relation to where the stone originates; the farther from the quarry, the higher the price. Expect to find natural color variations within each type of stone.

When selecting flagstone for outdoor paving, think of how it will be used. Formal entry and entertaining areas should be smooth surfaces, safely accommodating high heels. Patios that serve as sitting and dining areas also need a level surface for chairs and tables; select a stone with a fairly smooth surface. Also, some types of flagstones (notably sandstones) are porous and may be difficult to maintain under dining areas or near messy fruit trees. Some kinds can be slippery when wet.

Flagstones come in various thicknesses. The thinnest (also called veneer) range from $\frac{1}{4}$ to $\frac{3}{4}$ inch thick, and should be laid on a stout, 4-inch concrete slab. Thicker stones are typically laid in mortar atop a thinner concrete base (see page 119). Or, for a more casual look, consider setting thick stones in sand and adding plants between the joints.

Stone tiles

Many stone types are available precut in rectangular shapes. Popular tiles include those made from slate, sandstone, granite, quartzite, limestone, travertine (a pitted limestone that may be "filled"), and adoquin (a dense volcanic stone).

Outdoor tiles must be slip resistant. Naturally textured stones, including split slates and sandstones, are traditional choices. Other attractive slip-resistant textures are achieved by tumbling, sandblasting, flaming, or resplitting stone tiles.

Like porous ceramic tiles, those made from soft stones, such as limestone, may need to be sealed to protect against staining and acid damage. Since sealant products are constantly changing, the best approach is to discuss your specific

FLAGSTONES

Setting flagstones in soil (left) allows plants to grow between them, blending garden and patio. At once formal and earthy, Indian slate tiles (right) wrap an outdoor pavilion in warm, variegated tones.

needs with a knowledgeable stone supplier.

Stone tiles are usually laid in mortar with very thin grout lines, which gives them a stylish, formal look. However, beefier tiles—those about 1 inch or thicker—can be set in a sand base.

STONE TILES

Other stones

Fieldstone, river rocks, and pebbles are less expensive than flagstone and tile. These water-worn or glacier-ground stones form rustic pavings that make up in charm for what they lack in smoothness underfoot.

Smaller stones and pebbles can be either set in mortar or seeded into concrete. Large pieces may be laid directly on the soil as raised stepping-stones. An entire surface can be paved

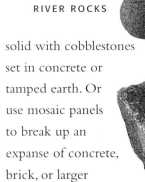

RIVER ROCKS

solid with cobblestones set in concrete or tamped earth. Or use mosaic panels to break up an expanse of concrete, brick, or larger flagstones.

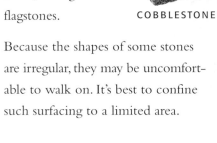

COBBLESTONE

Because the shapes of some stones are irregular, they may be uncomfortable to walk on. It's best to confine such surfacing to a limited area.

ceramic tile

Tile works well in both formal and informal garden situations. Its typically earthy tones blend well with natural colors outdoors, and the hard-fired pigments are permanent and nonfading. Because tile looks great indoors, too, it's a good flooring choice for an indoor room that adjoins a patio as well as for the patio itself.

Heavy tiles that are at least ¾ inch thick can be laid in a sand bed. However, the most stable bed for any tile is a 1-inch mortar bed over an existing concrete slab or a newly poured one (for details, see page 119).

Glazed or unglazed?

Glaze is a hard finish, usually colored, applied to the clay surface before final baking. Most bright, flashy tiles you see in displays are glazed.

Unless a special grit is added to glazed tiles, they can make treacherous footing when wet. For paving, it's best to use unglazed tiles, reserving their shiny, sporty counterparts for occasional accents or for raised planting beds.

Outdoor types

In cold climates, your tile choice must be freeze-thaw stable. So-called impervious and vitreous tiles, including quarry tiles and unglazed porcelain, are the best choices here. In milder climates, terra-cotta can hold its own.

Left: Gaining patina by age, this Mediterranean-style courtyard blends terra-cotta tile squares and diagonally set blue-glazed accents. The design centers on a vibrant tiled fountain.

Porcelain pavers can be made to resemble slate, limestone, and other stones, but come in straightforward pastel colors, too. While many tiles are polished, more slip-resistant textures include split (resembling slate) and sandblasted finishes and surfaces embossed with raised grids. Though 12-inch square pavers are standard, sizes range from 4- by 6-inch rectangles up through 24-inch squares.

Tough quarry tiles are made by the extrusion process (picture a giant pasta machine)—you can usually identify them by roller grooves in their backs. Though some quarry tiles are glazed, most come unglazed in natural clay colors of yellow, brown, rust, or red. Some exhibit "flashing," heat-produced shadings that vary from tile to tile. Typical sizes are 6 by 6, 8 by 8, and 12 by 12 inches. You'll also find some rectangles and a smattering of hexagons.

Translated from the Italian, terra-cotta means "cooked earth." But whether you see terra-cotta in antique French folk tile, hand-formed Mexican slabs (known as Saltillo tiles), or rustic Italian or Portuguese wares, the charm of this material lies in its very lack of consistency. Terra-cotta tiles come as squares, rectangles, hexagons, and octagons, as well as Moorish, ogee, and other interlocking shapes. These tiles are generally nonvitreous and highly absorbent, so they're iffy for outdoor use in cold climates.

To seal or not to seal?

Some unglazed tiles are sealed at the factory. Unsealed, unglazed units such as terra-cotta and some quarry tiles need to be sealed for protection against surface water and stains.

Surface or top sealers offer the most resistance to stains but darken tiles and can produce a sheen that you may or may not find appealing. These coatings must also be stripped and reapplied periodically.

Penetrating sealers soak into the tile instead of sitting on its surface. But they're not as protective as top sealers.

Sealer technology is changing all the time, and some proprietary formulas vary from region to region. Explain your intended use to a knowledgeable dealer and ask for a specific recommendation.

TERRA-COTTA TILES

PORCELAIN PAVERS

lumberyard primer

Because wood comes in so many sizes, species, and grades, a visit to a lumberyard or home center can be a daunting experience for the uninitiated. Busy salespeople may not be overly responsive if you're completely unfamiliar with lumber terms. But once you know a few basics, it's easier to get help with the fine points. Basic deck components are shown on page 117.

Below: Warm, natural wood decking floats out over a stately pond, providing the perfect platform for two comfy chairs.

Some basic lingo

First off, do you want softwood or hardwood? The terms don't really refer to the wood's relative hardness, but to the kind of tree from which it comes. Softwoods come from evergreens (conifers), hardwoods from broad-leafed (deciduous) trees. Decks are generally built from softwoods. However, new, more economical offerings of imported hardwoods such as ipé, mahogany, and plantation-grown teak (the boat builder's favorite) have recently entered the market. For more on these options, see pages 92–93.

A wood's properties are also determined by the part of the tree from which it comes. The inactive wood nearest the center of a living tree is called heartwood. Sapwood, next to the bark, contains the growth cells. Heartwood is more resistant to decay; sapwood is more porous and absorbs preservatives and other chemicals more readily.

Among heartwoods, the most decay-resistant and termite-proof species you can buy are redwood and cedar. This durability, combined with their natural beauty, makes them favorites for decking. On the other hand, they are softer, weaker, and more expensive than ordinary structural woods such as Douglas fir and Southern pine. To get the best of both worlds, most deck designers use fir or another structural wood for a deck's substructure, but redwood or cedar for decking, benches, and railings.

Grades

Lumber is sorted and graded at the mill. The higher the grade, the better the wood—and the more you will have to pay.

WESTERN RED CEDAR

Redwood is usually graded for its appearance and for the percentage of heartwood versus sapwood it contains. Among pure heartwoods, Clear All Heart is the best grade, followed by B Heart, Construction Heart, and Merchantable Heart.

Cedar grades, starting with the highest quality, are Architect Clear, Architect Knotty, and Custom Knotty. These grades don't indicate whether the lumber is heartwood or sapwood.

Pressure-treated lumber

Though redwood and cedar heartwoods resist decay and termites, other woods that contact the ground or trap water may quickly

rot and lose their strength. For this reason, less durable types such as Southern pine and Western hem-fir are often factory-treated with preservatives to protect them. These woods are generally less expensive and in many areas more readily available than redwood or cedar.

Compared with other softwoods, which are easy to cut and nail or screw, treated wood is often hard and brittle and is more likely to warp or twist. Moreover, some people object to its typically reddish or

Brightly painted decking links the porch to both furnishings and the traditional house siding.

greenish color (applying a stain can conceal it) and the staplelike incisions that usually cover it (some types come without these marks).

Because the preservatives used contain toxic metals, you should wear safety glasses and a dust mask when cutting treated lumber, and you should never burn it.

CONSTRUCTION HEART REDWOOD

CLEAR ALL HEART REDWOOD

ALASKA YELLOW CEDAR

PRESSURE-TREATED HEM-FIR

new decking options

Shrinking forests and dwindling supplies of quality lumber have nudged the development of both alternative wood products and engineered materials suitable for decks and other garden structures. All these offerings are intended for decking and railings only; typically, they sit atop a standard deck frame (see page 117) built from structural softwoods or pressure-treated lumber.

The tropical connection

Decks are going uptown by first heading below the equator. These new imported hardwoods can create a nearly furniture-grade look, especially when installed with invisible fasteners. Ipé is a beautiful, durable, rot-resistant wood that does not need to be finished. Cambara and meranti are two other choices. Plantation-grown mahogany and teak are also available in some areas.

Because they're harder and heavier than domestic decking woods, most tropicals come in a thinner "5⁄4" thickness (about 1 inch thick).

To find suitable hardwood products, you may have to do some shopping on the Internet or talk with local wood suppliers.

Ipé, a newly available tropical hardwood, adds an almost furniture-grade feel to this deck design.

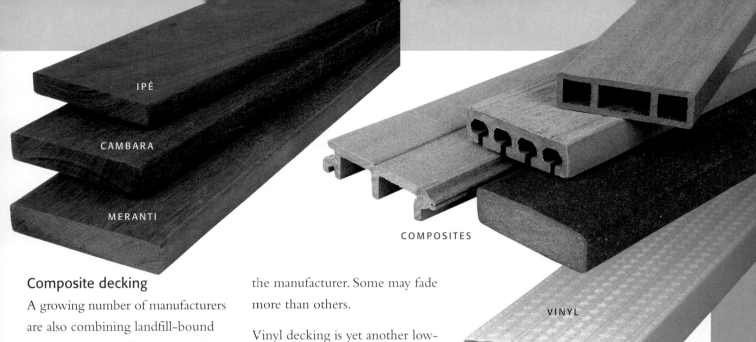

IPÉ

CAMBARA

MERANTI

COMPOSITES

VINYL

Composite decking

A growing number of manufacturers are also combining landfill-bound wood with waste plastic to produce so-called "wood-polymer composites." Though not meant for structural purposes, these weatherproof products can be used for both decking and railings. Besides the environmental angle, the big selling point is very low maintenance. For families with young children, these synthetic boards have the additional advantage of being splinter-free.

Composites come in both solid and hollow-core versions. Solid "boards" are simpler to deal with, but heavy; hollow types are lighter but fussier to install. Some composites look like real wood—at least from a distance. With others, it's best to simply view them as a new material. If you're not satisfied with the color choices, or if you would like your deck to match your house, most products can be stained or painted, as specified by

the manufacturer. Some may fade more than others.

Vinyl decking is yet another low-maintenance option, although one that offers a particularly non-traditional deck. Installation differs as well. In general, first an aluminum or vinyl track is installed across the joists, and then top pieces are snapped into place.

Manmade composite "boards" line both the deck and the built-in, wraparound bench above it.

heat it up!

Y_{ou} may want to consider adding some type of heating device to your new patio or deck to take the edge off the weather and increase the hours and days you can spend outdoors.

Fire Facts

A built-in fireplace is one way to go. But using a patio heater or fire pit is a simpler way to turn your outdoor room into a pleasant place to spend a brisk evening

You can buy a freestanding heater or install a more permanent gas or electric unit, which may prove more effective and less visible. A stainless steel mushroom heater, also known as an umbrella, radiates its warming rays from the top cylinder. A gas-fired directional heater mounts to a house's eaves, allowing it to throw heat efficiently without being intrusive.

Below: Almost invisible, this gas-fired directional heater warms the patio from its overhead perch.

Portable fire pits are popular for their ease of use and flexibility. You can enjoy them at home or take them on a picnic or to the beach. Fire pits sold in home-and-garden mail-order catalogs are generally made of copper; steel and other heat-resistant containers are also available. You can add an optional grill to some models. Most portable fire pits are fueled by wood or compressed logs; others run on propane or gel alcohol. Look for a fire pit with a sturdy wire-mesh spark screen for safety; or buy a mesh-walled model with an access door.

The three-legged chiminea is also popular, especially in South-western schemes. Its characteristic chimney may be integral to the base or sold separately. You can find chimineas in unadorned terra-cotta or in more decorative finishes and colors. Chimineas of cast iron, aluminum, steel, and copper are also sold. You'll need a spark screen for a wood-burning chiminea, and a heatproof mat if you're using it on a deck.

MUSHROOM HEATER

Barbecue basics

Do you like gas or charcoal? Many people prefer to cook with gas because it's so easy. Just turn on the burner and throw the meat on the grill. The best gas grills are made from high-quality stainless steel; they come in both built-in and freestanding models. Gas units are fueled either by natural gas or liquid propane (LP). Natural gas is more convenient—you don't need to buy and refill tanks—but more difficult to install because it requires a gas pipe that connects to your home's gas supply.

A steadfast group of grillers believe that charcoal produces better flavor, making it worth the extra work. A good charcoal grill is typically built of powder-coated or porcelain-enameled steel. The grate may be plated, to resist rust and clean up easily, or bare cast iron, which sears meat wonderfully but must be oiled to prevent rusting. A unit with a crank that raises and lowers the grate will make the heat easier to control.

STAND-ALONE GRILL

A handsome copper basin on a wrought-iron stand has a domed spark screen that swings open for adding firewood—or toasting marshmallows.

BUILT-IN GRILL

CHIMINEA

outdoor furniture

In the growing trend towards blurring indoor and outdoor distinctions, patio furnishings and fabrics play key roles.

Frames

The furnishings for your patio depend on the style of your outdoor room and its exposure to the weather. Spaces in temperate climes or under a sheltering arbor or roof can play host to more fragile materials than those more exposed.

Natural materials and textures are hallmarks of country and cottage styles. Wicker furniture recalls late 19th-century verandas and will

never go out of style; synthetic wicker can withstand more weather. Wrought iron chairs and benches also have a suitably old-fashioned appearance. Or try a bentwood creation.

Aiming for a classic look? It's often anchored by a good, stout wooden chair or bench. This kind of outdoor furniture is usually constructed from

Above: A colorful woven hammock adds its touch of tropical ease.

Left: Painted metal retro chairs, table, and umbrella combine to create a vintage gathering spot.

hardy, durable woods like teak or redwood. Adirondack chairs, sling chairs, and vintage metal chairs are classics, too. Designers are moving away from matched sets, mixing different woods and metals for variety.

Modern designs call for furniture with bright colors, sensuous and sculptural shapes, and retro modern style. These products are usually made of tough, all-weather materials like polypropylene or aluminum.

For gardens on the go, consider folding furniture, which can cluster atop loose materials or grass, then stow away when night falls. And don't forget another fair-weather friend: the hammock.

Fabrics

Fabrics soften the hard lines of your furnishings, completing the "outdoor room" look. Choose weatherproof fabrics if they'll be exposed for long periods. Synthetics like acrylic and, to a lesser degree, polyester, are tops; the best acrylics are treated with moisture- and stain-resistant coatings. Protected spots allow for a broader range of natural fabrics.

Exposure or not, pillows and throws provide a wider range of on-the-go accents; they're easy to stash when weather threatens.

COUNTRY STYLE

CLASSIC STYLE

CONTEMPORARY STYLE

lighting up the night

Safety, security, and decoration—all three are functions of outdoor lighting, and all can be achieved with a good lighting scheme. The only restriction is the need to keep both glare and wattage at a low level.

Low-voltage or line current?

When it's time to wire your landscape, you can choose either a standard 120-volt system or a low-voltage scheme.

Because low-voltage lights are safer, smaller, more energy efficient, and easier to install than 120-volt systems, they have become increasingly popular outdoors. Such systems use a transformer to step down household current to 12 volts, and thin, flexible cable to send the power to the fixtures. The cable can run along edgings or fence lines, be buried a few inches deep, or simply covered with mulch in a planting area. Although low-voltage fixtures lack the "punch" of line-current fixtures, their output is sufficient for most outdoor applications.

The standard 120-volt system still has some advantages outdoors. The buried cable and metallic fixtures give the installation a look of permanence; light can be projected a greater distance; and 120-volt outlets accept power tools and patio heaters.

Fixtures and bulbs

Standard outdoor fixtures range from well lights and other portable uplights to spread lights that illuminate paths or bridges and downlights designed to be anchored to the house wall, eaves, or trees.

Most outdoor fixtures are made of bronze, cast or extruded aluminum, copper, or plastic. But you can also find decorative stone, concrete, porcelain, and wood fixtures (redwood, cedar, and teak weather best). Sizes vary. When evaluating fixtures, look for gaskets, high-quality components at joints and pivot points, and locking devices for aiming the fixtures.

Low-voltage halogen MR-16 bulbs are popular for accenting; PAR spotlights are best to light trees or wide areas. Flood lights, available in

Left: Colorful paper lanterns lend their soft amber glow, and strands of white Christmas lights stuffed into Chinese baskets add sparkle.

DAYLIGHT SENSORS

OUTDOOR TIMER

VINTAGE CANDLE LANTERN

MOTION SENSOR FIXTURE

MR-16 BULB

PAR BULB

LOW-VOLTAGE CABLE AND UPLIGHTS

TRANSFORMER

incandescent and mercury-vapor versions, are for security purposes only; they're too wide and too glare-prone for garden accenting.

Some fixtures and bulbs are just for fun. Decorative rope lights help outline trees and structures and lend sparkle to your landscape. Strings of low-wattage party lights add a festive flair. And don't forget non-electric sources, too, like hurricane lamps, candle lanterns, or solar path lights.

Get control

How can you set up landscape or security lights to take care of themselves? A timer is one solution. Two other options are daylight-sensitive photocells and motion-sensor fixtures or add-ons.

Daylight sensors are simply photocells that react to daylight. When it's dark, the photocell sends power to the light fixture it's connected to; come dawn, the sensor opens the circuit, shutting down the fixture.

Like photocells, motion sensors can be purchased alone or integrated into a fixture that houses one or more floodlights. Some sensors have adjustable ranges and can be set to remain on for varying lengths of time.

If your outdoor lighting circuit begins indoors, you can control it with the same switches and timers you'd use there. But if your system connects outdoors, choose a hardier outdoor timer, as shown above.

ROPE LIGHT

How to DO IT

AS MUCH FUN AS IT IS to daydream about
that new outdoor space you're going to create, careful
planning is what will make the dream happen. That's
where this chapter helps. Dig right in for both solid
design principles and a guided walk through the planning process. When you've finished, you should have
working drawings in hand. Use them to communicate
with landscape professionals or, if you're so inclined,
to build the project yourself.

Taking *Stock*

THE PATH TO A GREAT new patio or deck begins right outside your door. On the following pages, we take a look at basic site strategies and consider some important weather factors. Then we show you how to make a detailed base map of your property. Want to take a quick poll of your yard's problems and possibilities? See "Twenty Questions," on page 105.

How's your weather?

Your site's exposure to sun, wind, rain, and snow can limit its potential as an enjoyable outdoor room. Microclimates (weather pockets created by localized conditions) can also make a big difference. Studying them might prompt you to relocate your proposed deck or patio, extend its dimensions, or change its design. You also may be able to moderate the impact of the weather with the addition of an overhead structure, walls, screens, or plantings.

In general, a site that faces north is cold because it receives little sun. A south-facing patio is usually warm because it gets daylong sun. An east-facing patio is likely to be cool, receiving only morning sun. A west-facing patio can be unbearably hot because it gets the full force of the afternoon sun; in late afternoon, a harsh glare also may be a problem.

Chilly winds may blow, but this cozy corner has it covered. Stacked adobe walls back a built-in hearth and cheery chiminea.

SUN PATH

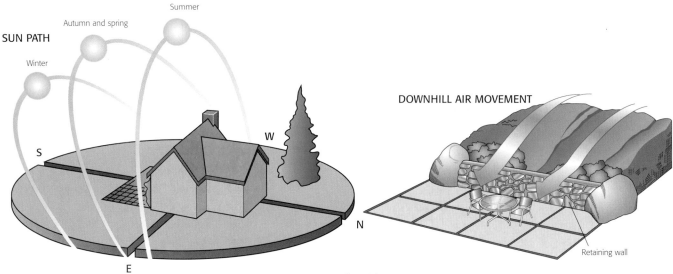

Summer

Autumn and spring

Winter

S

W

N

E

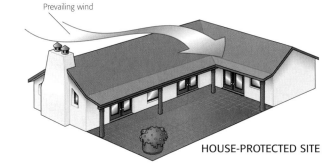

DOWNHILL AIR MOVEMENT

Retaining wall

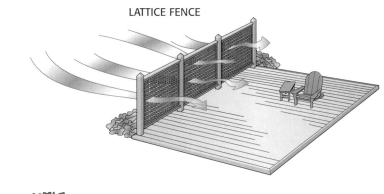

Prevailing wind

HOUSE-PROTECTED SITE

LATTICE FENCE

DECIDUOUS PLANTINGS

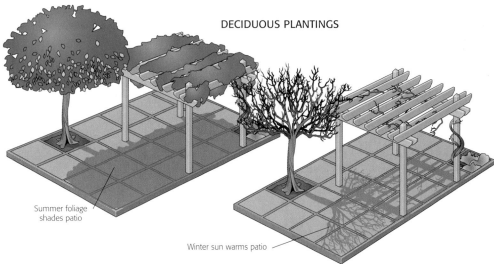

Summer foliage shades patio

Winter sun warms patio

Another factor to consider is the sun's path during the year. As the sun passes over your house, it makes an arc that changes slightly every day, becoming higher in summer and lower in winter. Changes in the sun's path not only give us long days in summer and short ones in winter, but also alter shade patterns in your yard.

Remember that cold air flows down–hill like water, puddles in basins, and can be dammed by walls or fences. Note any spots where cold air settles and frost is heavy.

If, in assessing your climate, you learn that winter storms generally blow out of the northeast, you may want to locate your patio or deck where it will take less of a buffeting from the weather. Fences and walls can help, but strategically placed barrier plantings also block strong winds, while allowing gentle breezes to pass through. Deciduous trees can shelter a patio from hot sun in summer, yet admit welcome rays on crisp winter days, when their leaves are gone.

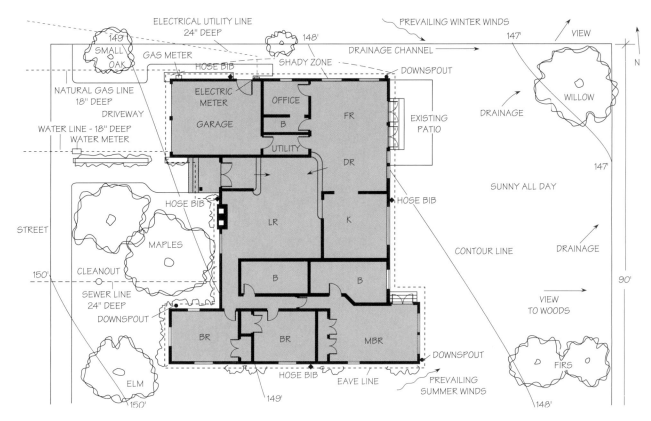

ELECTRICAL UTILITY LINE
24" DEEP

PREVAILING WINTER WINDS

VIEW

149'

SMALL
OAK

GAS METER

HOSE BIB

148'

SHADY ZONE

DRAINAGE CHANNEL

DOWNSPOUT

147'

N

WILLOW

NATURAL GAS LINE
18" DEEP

DRIVEWAY

ELECTRIC
METER

GARAGE

OFFICE

B

FR

EXISTING
PATIO

DRAINAGE

147'

WATER LINE - 18" DEEP
WATER METER

UTILITY

DR

STREET

HOSE BIB

LR

K

HOSE BIB

SUNNY ALL DAY

CONTOUR LINE

DRAINAGE

90'

150'

MAPLES

CLEANOUT

B

B

VIEW
TO WOODS

SEWER LINE
24" DEEP

DOWNSPOUT

BR

BR

MBR

DOWNSPOUT

FIRS

ELM

150'

149'

HOSE BIB

EAVE LINE

PREVAILING
SUMMER WINDS

148'

A SAMPLE BASE MAP

Making a base map

Even if you've lived with a landscape for years, mapping it can be a way to make some interesting discoveries about what you thought was familiar territory. Use your observations about your site to produce a base map like the one shown above. Later, slip the base map under tracing paper to sketch designs to your heart's content.

A complete mapping kit includes T-square, triangles, compass, circle template, architect's scale, eraser, and 50-foot tape measure.

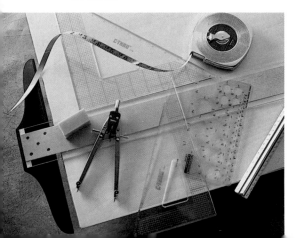

You can save yourself some time by obtaining dimensions, gradients, and relevant structural details from your deed map, house plans, or a contour map of your lot. If you don't have these, see if they're available through your city hall, county office, title company, or bank.

To draw your base map (and later, any final plan), you'll need 24- by 36-inch graph paper (¼-inch scale, unless the size of your property requires ⅛-inch scale), an art gum eraser, a straightedge, several pencils, and a pad of tracing paper. Optional are a drafting board, a T-square, one or more triangles, a compass, a circle template, and an architect's scale. For taking measurements in the existing landscape, choose either a 50- or

100-foot tape measure; anything shorter is exasperating to use and can lead to inaccurate measurements.

If you can use a personal computer, don't overlook the growing collection of drawing and landscape-planning software programs. Unlike earlier CAD programs aimed at professionals, some of the newer offerings are designed for the more limited needs and budgets of homeowners.

Outline your property accurately and to scale, and mark its dimensions on the base map. Also show your house to scale within the property. Note all exterior doors, the height of all lower-story windows, and all overhangs. Mark the locations of hose bibbs, downspouts, and any drainage tiles, drainpipes, or catch basins.

TWENTY
Questions

1. Where's north on your property? Where are the patterns of sun and shade? How do they change during the day?

2. What is the direction of the prevailing wind? What microclimates (daily breezes, cold spots, etc.) require special attention?

3. Check your site for high and low spots. Would grading be required? Or a retaining wall?

4. Is there adequate drainage? Where does the water go? Note any point where drainage is impeded (leaving soggy soil) and any place where runoff could cause erosion.

5. What are the setback allowances in your area? Are there other code or deed restrictions on outdoor structures?

6. Do any underground utility lines run through the area? What about the sewer line or septic tank? If you're contemplating a patio roof or elevated deck, identify any overhead lines.

7. Are there views you'd like to feature? Or some you'd like to screen? Also take into account views into your yard from nearby houses or streets.

8. Is noise a problem?

9. Who will use the patio or deck, and in what seasons? Will the area be used for entertaining?

10. How will the patio or deck be accessed from the house, or from the yard or garden?

11. What style do you prefer: formal or informal? How does that style relate to your home's exterior and present landscaping?

12. Do you prefer decking (wood or composite) or a masonry hardscape? Or would you like a combination of the two?

13. What other structures would you like: fence, walls, hedge, arbor, gazebo? Do you want built-in seating?

14. How about other amenities: line-voltage or low-voltage lighting, fireplace or other heat source, a built-in barbecue or outdoor kitchen, home-entertainment components?

15. Will the site feature a swimming pool? What about other water features: wall fountain, garden pool, waterfall, or stream? How will plumbing reach these features?

16. What existing plantings should be saved? What new plantings should be added? Do you need to add minisprinklers or a drip system? What about wooden planters, containers, or a trellis?

17. Do you need storage? A potting table or shed? Cabinets for an outdoor kitchen? Storage space for lawn furniture or firewood?

18. Are you willing and able to do any, or all, of the prep work or building yourself?

19. How long do you have to complete the project?

20. What budget figure do you have in mind?

You'll want to take inventory of your present yard in order to judge how you want to change it. Used with your base map, your responses to the questions at left will also provide a good starting point for a discussion with landscape designers, contractors, or suppliers. Write your answers on a separate sheet of paper, adding any other preferences or dislikes that come to mind. Then gather your notes, any clippings you've collected, and a copy of your base map, and you're ready to begin planning your new deck or patio.

What are *Your Options?*

SOME FOLKS REGARD a patio or deck as a simple rectangle off the back door. But why not consider a succession of small patios and level changes connected by steps, or a secluded "getaway" deck to make use of an attractive corner of your property? Enclosed entry courtyards are another growing trend. Perhaps you could even reclaim a forsaken side yard. Here's a tour of the possibilities.

Wide brick landings make inviting rest stops along a cascading set of stairs.

Basic backyard patios

The standard backyard rectangle doesn't have to be boring. Edgings, raised beds, and maybe a gentle curve or two can customize and soften your design. Containers or hanging plants and other amenities can also help transform your space.

L- and U-shaped spaces

A house with an L or U shape is perfect for a patio or deck. Surrounding house walls already form an enclosure; a privacy screen and a decorative structure overhead (such as an arbor, pergola, or even a simple roof) complete the "outdoor room." Often such a site can be accessed gracefully from several parts of the house.

Wraparounds

A flat lot is a natural candidate for a wraparound patio. It enlarges the apparent size of the house, while allowing access from any room along its course. If there's a gentle grade, rise above it with a slightly elevated deck, which the Japanese call an engawa.

Detached sites

Perfect for serving as a quiet retreat, a detached patio or deck can be built on either a flat or a sloping lot and looks very much at home in a casual or cottage-garden landscape. Create access to it with a direct walkway or a meandering garden path. A patio roof, privacy screen, or small fountain can make such a space even more enjoyable. Or consider building a formal gazebo on the site.

Multilevel decks and patios

A large lot, especially one with changes in elevation, can often accommodate decks and patios on different levels and linked by steps or pathways. Such a scheme works well when your outdoor space must serve many purposes. Meandering paths, augmented by benches and planting beds along the way, encourage a leisurely stroll.

Rooftop and balcony sites

No open space in the yard? Look up. A garage rooftop adjacent to a second-story living area might be ideal for a sunny outdoor lounging space. Or consider a small balcony patio with a built-in bench and planter box. Just be sure your existing structure can take the weight of additional wood or masonry (consult an architect or structural engineer), and plan for adequate drainage.

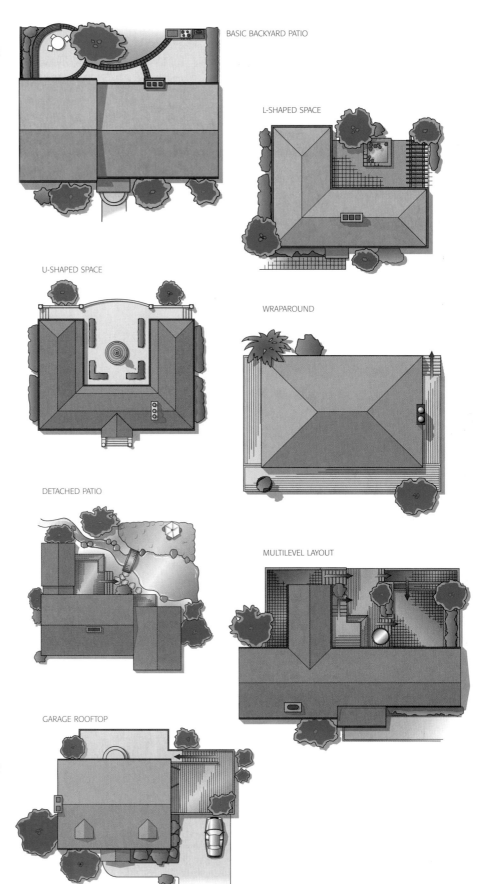

BASIC BACKYARD PATIO

L-SHAPED SPACE

U-SHAPED SPACE

WRAPAROUND

DETACHED PATIO

MULTILEVEL LAYOUT

GARAGE ROOFTOP

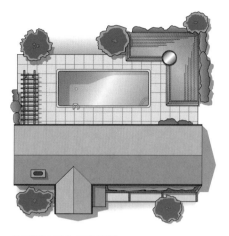

SWIMMING POOL SURROUND

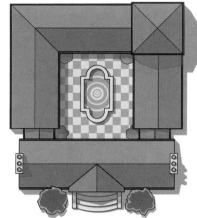

INTERIOR COURTYARD

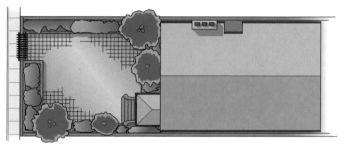

ENTRY PATIO

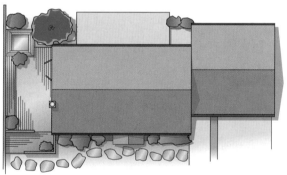

SIDE YARD SPACE

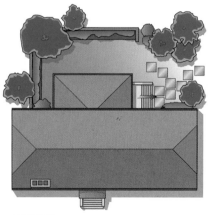

BACK PORCH

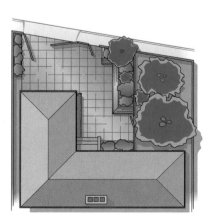

RECLAIMED DRIVEWAY

Swimming pool surrounds

When the focus of patio living is a swimming pool, the setting can be formal and rectangular or natural, with the pool blending into an informal landscape. Surround the pool with skidproof masonry (light colors are cooler underfoot) and/ or low-level decking. A patio roof, dining and kitchen area, and spa are effective additions.

Entry patios

Pavings, plantings, and perhaps a trickling fountain enclosed by a privacy wall can transform an ordinary entry path or front lawn into a private oasis. If local codes prohibit building high solid walls, try using a hedge, arbor, or trellis to let in light and air while screening off the street.

Side yard spaces

A neglected side yard may be just the spot for a sheltered outdoor sitting area. And what about a container-grown herb garden or a sunny breakfast deck off a cramped kitchen and accessed by way of French or sliding doors? If you're subject to fence height restrictions, use an arbor or overhead structure to protect privacy.

Interior courtyards

If you're designing a new home, consider incorporating a private interior courtyard, or atrium. Indoor-outdoor links are key here: think French or sliding doors—or, in warm climates, whole walls that slide or fold open.

Porches and sunrooms

Where summers swelter, the classic porch still evokes a traditional kind of indoor-outdoor living. In bug country, however, screened porches or sunrooms make sense. Some sunrooms can be opened up when the sun shines and battened down when hard winds blow.

Reclaimed driveways

Your driveway can double as a masonry patio. Concrete turf blocks can support car traffic but yield a softer appearance than plain asphalt or concrete; planting small spaces between pavers or flagstones achieves the same result. Enclosed by a gate, the front drive becomes an entry courtyard.

Existing slabs

If you have an old slab, you can either demolish it and start over, or put a new surface on top. An existing concrete slab, unless heavily damaged, can serve admirably as a base for brick, pavers, tile, or stone; you can also top-dress it with colored or stamped concrete. Or break up the old slab (literally) with a series of new planting pockets. Yet another option: construct a low-level deck atop part, or all, of the slab.

Top right: Deep roof eaves cap a wrap-around wood deck, forming the perfect porch for two Adirondack chairs.

Bottom right: Lush plantings—some in containers, some in jack-hammered holes—help reclaim an old asphalt driveway.

Design
Basics

WITH YOUR BASE MAP DRAWN and some options in mind, you can begin trying out your ideas and determining the style of your patio or deck. As you brainstorm, you'll begin to work out the use areas and circulation patterns and make general decisions about which kinds of structures and amenities you'll need. You may also wish to review some classic design guidelines (see page 113).

What's your style?

One early design decision you should make is whether you want a formal or informal outdoor environment. The style you choose should be compatible with the architecture of your house and appropriate to your climate.

Formal landscapes are symmetrical, with straight lines, geometric patterns, and clearly established balance; they often include sheared hedges, wall fountains, pools, or outdoor sculptures. Paving might be of mortared brick, cut stone, or ceramic tile.

Poured concrete lends a more industrial look to a formal garden. Seeded-aggregate, smooth-troweled, or textured concrete are more modern in feel.

Informal styles, on the other hand, tend to favor curves, asymmetry, and apparent randomness; adjacent plantings are usually naturalistic, too. Masonry units, if used, are set in more

Formal as can be, this patio joins cobblestone paving, trimmed hedges, potted plants and topiary, plus classic wood furnishings.

casual sand beds (see pages 118–119). Flagstones, river rocks, and gravel can lend a native, nature-oriented look. Wooden decks seem at home in just about any informal setting.

Raked gravel that imitates swirling water, carefully placed boulders, a spill fountain, and a hidden garden bench or bridge are all trademarks of an Asian-style garden.

You can learn a lot about style by studying gardens that you visit or see in magazines, as well as those illustrated throughout this book. Here are some stylistic themes that are part of a wide range you may encounter:

- Period (as in Georgian, Victorian)

- Mediterranean

- Southwestern

- Cottage-garden

- Tropical

- Asian

- Avant-garde

- Rustic

- Natural

- Eclectic

Top right: A cottage-garden scheme blends broken-concrete chunks with a mix of ground covers between. There's just enough hardscape for a bench and table.

Bottom right: This Moroccan-style courtyard features marble tile, lush plantings, and trickling water that flows from a wall fountain to a stair-stepped water channel.

Define use areas

Ready to start planning? First focus on your family's needs and activities. Think about the way you live, making a list of what's most important to you (if you have children, get their input, too). Then, if you need to compromise, you can compromise on the less important things.

Next, review your yard's assets. Can your plan capitalize on a fine view? Perhaps your design can take advantage of a sunny southern exposure or an impressive garden tree.

Consider also your yard's handicaps. Is your lot on a steep slope? How much of the lot is exposed to street noise or a neighbor's view? If you're rethinking an existing patio or deck, ask yourself whether it opens off the wrong room, gets too much sun or shade, or lacks sufficient space.

Now get ready to try out your ideas. For each design attempt, use a separate sheet of tracing paper placed over your base map, sketching rough circular or oval shapes ("balloons") to represent the location and approximate size of each use area. For an example, see the balloon drawing above right.

As you sketch, concentrate on logical placement. For example, are you locating a children's play area in full view of your living area? Is the private sunning spot you envision easily accessible from the master bedroom?

A BALLOON DRAWING

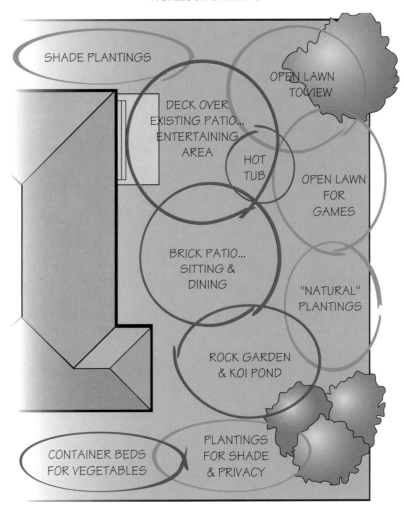

Design with shapes

When your experiments with diagrams have resulted in a rough sketch, lay a clean sheet of tracing paper on top of it. On this sheet, and on as many more as you need, begin roughing in the various building blocks of the design—paving, enclosing walls or hedges, arbors, benches, and perhaps a pool or spa.

At this point, keep in mind two tricks of the landscape designer. First, work with clear simple shapes; second,

relate those shapes to the lines of your house. A design that's made of familiar shapes such as squares, rectangles, triangles, and circles is easier to understand than one filled with abstract lines.

Vary the sizes of the shapes you work with, but don't use too many little shapes or you will end up with a busy design. Add a curve, perhaps, to connect two rectangular spaces, or use a diagonal line to emphasize the longest dimension in a small garden.

GUIDES
to Good Design

■ **Meet your needs.** Your design should be able to accommodate your family's favorite activities, from relaxation and casual gatherings to children's games, barbecues, and entertaining.

■ **Protect privacy.** As an extension of your indoor living space, your patio should offer the same feeling of privacy as interior rooms do, but with no sense of confinement. Building an elevated deck, for example, can open as many un- pleasant views as attractive ones—and expose you to view, as well. Do you need to add screens, arbors, or plantings to remedy the problem? Could an ivy-draped wall and a trickling fountain help buffer unwanted noise?

■ **Be aware of safety.** Patio paving materials have different properties. For example, some become slippery when wet; others are too sharp or uneven for children's games. Passage from house to patio and from deck to garden must be safe and unobstructed. Adequate lighting should be provided at steps and along garden paths.

■ **Use color.** As in a beautiful indoor room, colors should be placed in a coordinated relationship to one another. Brick, adobe, wood, and stone have distinctive, generally earthy colors. Con- crete has more industrial overtones, but can be softened with aggregate, stamping and staining, or integral color. Even plants on or around your

Here, wavy lines reply to a beat of straight lines. This design is all about rhythm; one of the owners is a jazz guitarist.

patio or deck should contribute harmonious tones. Remember that all foliage is not simply "green"; the range of shades is really very large.

■ **Think transitions.** A patio or deck should entice people outdoors. So be sure to consider the transition from the inside of your house to the outside. Wide French or sliding glass doors make the outdoors look inviting and also help the interior space expand psychologically.

■ **Attend to details.** Paying a little extra attention to the fine points of a patio or deck can add a lot to its style and substance. Improve the workmanship of the railings and trim, and the whole deck looks more intensively crafted.

Experienced landscape pros employ several criteria to ensure that a deck or patio is useful and comfortable and that it also complements its surroundings visually. When planning, you may wish to review the specifics at left.

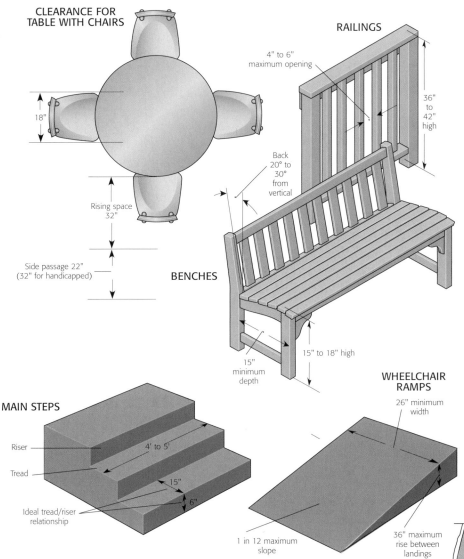

CLEARANCE FOR TABLE WITH CHAIRS

18"

Rising space 32"

Side passage 22"
(32" for handicapped)

RAILINGS

4" to 6" maximum opening

36" to 42" high

Back 20° to 30° from vertical

BENCHES

15" to 18" high

15" minimum depth

MAIN STEPS

Riser

Tread

4' to 5'

15"

6"

Ideal tread/riser relationship

WHEELCHAIR RAMPS

26" minimum width

1 in 12 maximum slope

36" maximum rise between landings

Examine circulation patterns

Also consider foot-traffic connections between use areas, as well as from individual areas to the house and yard. Will too much traffic be channeled through areas meant for relaxation? Can guests move easily from the entertainment area to the garden? Can the lawn mower be moved from the tool shed to the lawn without disturbing someone's repose?

One way to improve access to and from the house is to add a door. But if you have to open up a wall to improve circulation, be sure you won't end up with a traffic pattern that runs through the middle of a room.

When planning, you'll need to allow at least the established minimum clearances; for guidelines, see the illustrations at left and below.

BENCH CLEARANCE

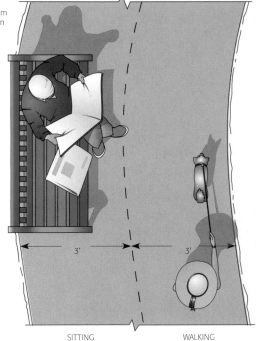

SITTING WALKING

3' 3'

PATHWAY CLEARANCE

2' to 3'

SERVICE PATHWAY

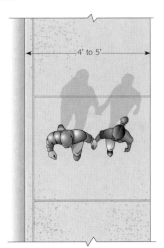

4' to 5'

MAIN PATHWAY

MAKING
a Mock-up

If you are having difficulty visualizing the finished landscape or can't quite decide on the specifics of certain elements, you may wish to mock up the design on your actual property. Seeing an approximation of the layout in the form of stakes, strings, and other markings can help you determine the exact dimensions necessary for features such as decks, terraces, and walks.

To outline paving areas, patio or deck construction, pathways, and planting beds with straight or gently curved lines, mark each corner with a short stake and connect the stakes with string. Use taller stakes to mark fences and walls. Tall stakes can also represent trees or elements like fountains, sculpture, or posts for overhead construction.

If your design has curved and free-form shapes, snake a garden hose to lay out the lines to your liking. Limestone or gypsum can be used to mark free-form designs; so can spray paint. Powdered chalk in different colors is useful if you have overlapping elements. To revise your plan, simply turn the powder over into the soil and start again.

Stakes and strings (top left and right) block out straight lines. For curves, use a garden hose (bottom)—here, we're marking the shape with spray paint.

Nuts
& Bolts

WHETHER OR NOT YOU INTEND TO BUILD a patio or deck yourself, a basic understanding of the materials and methods involved can be useful. A working knowledge of these details, plus some background on grading and drainage options, can help gauge your do-it-yourself zeal and zero in on material costs. You'll also be able to communicate more easily with landscape pros.

Deck details

If grade or drainage presents a problem, or if you simply prefer the look and feel of a wooden surface, a deck may be your choice.

A deck can be freestanding or, as shown on the facing page, attached to the house via a horizontal ledger. The structure is designed with a stacking principle in mind, with each new layer perpendicular to the one below. Concrete footings secure precast piers or poured, tubular pads, which in turn support vertical wooden posts. Horizontal beams span the posts; joists run perpendicular to ledger and beams.

The decking itself, typically 2 by 4 or 2 by 6 lumber or composite, is nailed or screwed to the joists. Be sure that your decking is at least 1 inch below any door sill and that there are $\frac{1}{8}$- to $\frac{3}{16}$-inch drainage gaps between boards. The decking needn't run directly across the

This owner-built deck features dark-stained cedar, built-in steps and benches, and an enclosed skirt that matches the house siding.

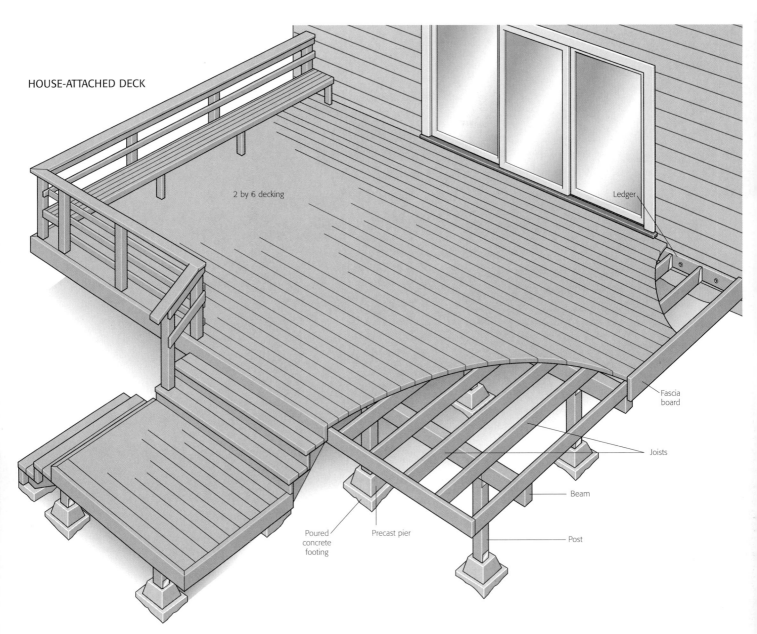

HOUSE-ATTACHED DECK

2 by 6 decking

Ledger

Fascia board

Joists

Beam

Post

Poured concrete footing

Precast pier

joists; you might also opt for a diagonal pattern.

Overhead structures, benches, railings, and steps are often integral to a deck's framing. While it may be feasible to add these later, it's simplest to design and build the whole project at once.

In a deck's structure, the size and spacing of each component affect the members above and below. Minimum and maximum sizes are stipulated by your building code. Posts taller than about 3 feet may require bracing, especially in areas prone to earthquakes or high winds. Elevated decks require railings (again, specified by local code).

Fascia boards, skirts, and other trim details help add a custom touch to the basic structure. For a closer look at options for decking lumber, see pages 90–93.

Are you planning a rooftop deck? It must be sloped above an impermeable membrane—a job for a roofing contractor.

Patio profiles

Most patios are constructed in one of two ways—with a poured concrete slab or base or atop a bed of clean, packed sand.

A concrete slab suits heavy-use areas and formal designs. The slab should be at least 4 inches thick (see drawing on facing page, top) and, for better drainage, underlaid with 2 to 8 inches of gravel. Welded wire mesh helps reinforce the structure. Wooden

Gray gravel forms a casual and comfortable base for dining, gardening, or—in the orange cat's case—some serious snoozing.

forms define the slab's shape; they're usually removed once the concrete has set. Wet concrete is poured into the forms like batter into a cake pan. While still plastic, the concrete is leveled and the surface is smoothed.

A thinner concrete pad, typically about 3 inches thick, can serve as the base for masonry units such as brick, ceramic tile, or flagstones set in mortar (see drawing on facing page, bottom left).

A sand bed (see drawing on facing page, bottom right) is popular for casual brick, pavers, and cobblestone

patios and walks. Layers of gravel and landscape fabric provide drainage and stability; damp sand is then carefully leveled—or "screeded"—on top. Paving units go atop the screeded bed, and then additional sand is cast over the surface and worked into joints to lock units in place. Edgings help define the patio and keep units from shifting.

Whatever surface you choose, you should slope it a minimum of 1 inch per 8 feet for drainage. Walkways can be angled slightly so that water is channeled away.

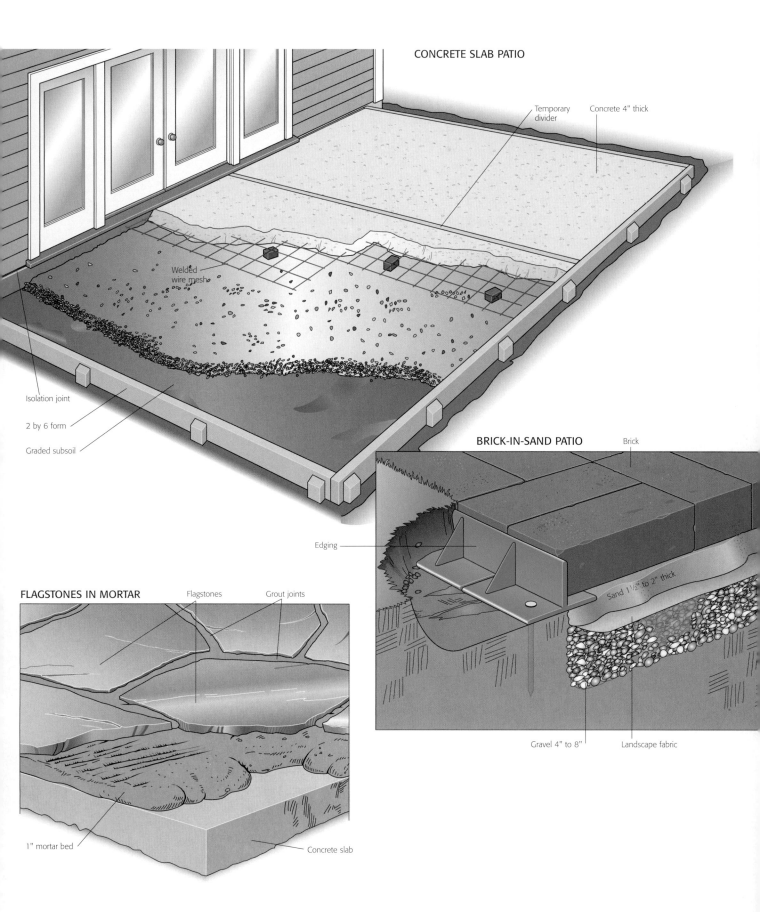

CONCRETE SLAB PATIO

Temporary divider

Concrete 4" thick

Welded wire mesh

Isolation joint

2 by 6 form

Graded subsoil

BRICK-IN-SAND PATIO

Brick

Edging

Sand 1½" to 2" thick

Gravel 4" to 8"

Landscape fabric

FLAGSTONES IN MORTAR

Flagstones

Grout joints

1" mortar bed

Concrete slab

OBSERVING
the Lay of the Land

Whenever you can fit any landscape element into the existing topography with little or no disturbance of the soil, you save time, effort, and expense.

However, that isn't always possible. Sometimes the existing topography has inherent problems, or you realize you must alter it in order to accommodate your ideal design. Then you must grade the site—reshape it by removing soil, adding soil, or both. In most cases, it's best to consult a landscape architect or soils engineer.

If your property lies on a slope so steep that without skillful grading and terracing it would remain unstable and useless, consider constructing one or more retaining walls.

The safest way to build a retaining wall is to place it at the bottom of a gentle slope, if space permits, and fill in behind it. That way you won't disturb the stability of the soil. Otherwise, the hill can be held either with a single high wall or with a series of low walls forming graceful terraces.

A steep slope becomes a virtue when tamed by stone retaining walls, steps, and lush planting beds.

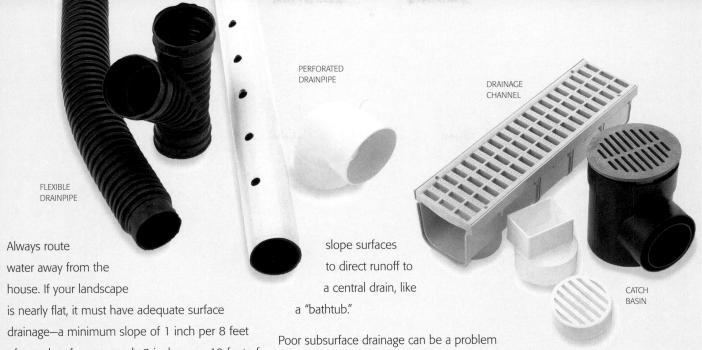

FLEXIBLE
DRAINPIPE

PERFORATED
DRAINPIPE

DRAINAGE
CHANNEL

CATCH
BASIN

DOWNSPOUT ADAPTER

Always route water away from the house. If your landscape is nearly flat, it must have adequate surface drainage—a minimum slope of 1 inch per 8 feet of paved surface, or nearly 3 inches per 10 feet of unpaved ground. Steeper gradients are better for slow-draining, heavier soils.

Where property slopes towards the house, you may need to shore it up with a retaining wall and slope surfaces to direct runoff to a central drain, like a "bathtub."

Poor subsurface drainage can be a problem where the water table is close to the surface. Plastic drainpipes, drainage channels, and catch basins can be the answer in many situations. But to plan and install a drainage system for a problem hillside, get professional help.

"BATHTUB" PATIO

Retaining wall

Perforated
drainpipe

Dry well

Catch basin

Downspout

Putting It *All Together*

ONCE YOU'VE DECIDED how you want to use your outdoor space, what type of structure will accomplish this best, and what alterations of gradient are required, you're ready to firm up your plan. This rendering is the end result of the design process; use it for fine-tuning, for estimating materials, and when talking with landscaping professionals.

The final plan

To create your plan, you'll need the same basic tools you used to draw your base map (see page 104). Most designers create a "plan" view and one or more "elevations." (A plan view is the classic bird's-eye view of the layout as seen from above; an elevation shows how the scene would look to a person standing nearby.)

Place a clean sheet of tracing paper over your base map. Draw carefully and label all features clearly. Complex structures, such as spas, walls, or overheads, may call for additional details or a cross-section (a slice through an object, rendered at an even larger scale).

If you have a knack for design, there's no reason why you can't develop a working plan. If pros will be relying on your plan for information or complex details, however, it's wise to have at least a brief consultation with a landscape architect or designer.

Used brick paving, cool pool, rose arbor, and formal furnishings—here's where all the elements come together.

NEED *Help?*

Who is the right advisor to help you adapt, develop, or build your patio or deck? Here are some of the people who can offer assistance, along with a brief look at what they do.

- **Architects and landscape architects.** These professionals have a bachelor's or master's degree in architecture or landscape architecture. They're trained to create designs that are structurally sound, functional, and esthetically pleasing. They know construction materials, can negotiate bids from contractors, and can supervise the actual work. Many are willing to give a simple consultation, either in their offices or at your home, for a modest fee.

- **Landscape and building designers.** Landscape designers usually have a landscape architect's education and training but not a state license. Building designers, whether licensed (by the American Institute of Building Designers) or unlicensed, may offer design help along with construction services.

- **Structural and soils engineers.** If you're planning to build a structure on an unstable or steep lot or where heavy wind or loads come into play, you should consult an engineer. A soils engineer evaluates soil conditions and establishes design specifications for foundations. A structural engineer, often working with the calculations a soils engineer provides, designs foundation piers and footings to suit the site. Engineers also provide wind- and load-stress calculations as required.

- **Contractors.** Licensed general and landscape contractors specialize in construction (landscape contractors specialize in garden construction), although some have design experience as well. They usually charge less for design work than landscape architects do, but their design skills may be limited by a construction point of view. Contractors may do the work themselves or assume responsibility for ordering materials, hiring qualified subcontractors, and seeing that the job is completed according to contract.

A wooden boardwalk zigzags its way to a driftwood arbor overlooking the water.

Can you do it yourself?

If you're a skilled weekend carpenter, you should have no problem building a simple deck or overhead structure, such as an arbor. The trick is to proceed at a workable pace, one deliberate step at a time. However, certain conditions may require professional help.

A deck on unstable soil, sand, mud, or water needs special foundations for support—and perhaps the advice of an engineer as well as a builder. A high-level deck or one on a steep hillside also involves special design methods and may be too difficult for a do-it-yourselfer to build.

Concrete work, while straightforward, can present a logistical and physical challenge. The trick is to start small, dividing the work into stages that you and one or two other people can handle. If your job is complex or requires a large, continuous pour, leave it to the pros.

Patios assembled from smaller units, such as bricks or stones, can be built at a more leisurely pace. But be advised that, for the average weekend mason, the constant lifting, mixing, and shoveling may take their toll.

If you'd like more details on the step-by-step process of building decks, patios, or related outdoor structures, take a look at the Sunset titles *The Complete Deck Book; Walks, Walls & Patio Floors; Fences, Walls & Gates; Trellises & Arbors;* or *Patio Roofs.*

AFTER

BEFORE

A tiny, dreary backyard slab (inset) gained new life with containers, hanging baskets, a trellis, and shelving for shade-loving plants. Variegated foliage and light-colored blooms help brighten the space.

Dollars and cents

So, how much will your new patio project cost? A lot depends on the materials you choose and where you live in relation to where those materials come from. The farther you are from the source, the more you'll pay.

One money-saving strategy is, of course, to provide as much of the labor as you can yourself. Even if you're not up to heavy construction or skilled brickwork, you might discover a latent talent for site prepping or demolition, form building, posthole digging, painting, or simply moving materials via wheelbarrow from point A to point B.

A BUILDER'S *Checklist*

The lists below can help you plan the sequence of tasks involved in building the basic patio or deck. Depending on the size of your job and the materials you select, you may need to alter the suggested order somewhat. Manufacturers' instructions offer additional guidelines.

Brick or pavers in sand

1. Lay out the site

2. Grade

3. Provide for drainage, if required

4. Install edgings

5. Spread out gravel bed

6. Screed sand bed atop gravel

7. Place units, tamp them level

8. Cut and install border pieces

9. Sweep sand into joints

10. Mist the patio surface; add more sand

Concrete slab (or units atop slab)

1. Lay out the site

2. Grade

3. Provide for drainage, if required

4. Install wooden forms

5. Spread out gravel subbase

6. Add steel reinforcement, if required

7. Mix and pour concrete

8. Screed concrete

9. Float surface smooth or add other texture

10. Cure concrete for several days

CORDLESS DRIVER/DRILL

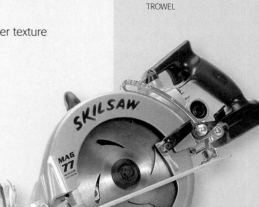

MASON'S TROWEL

Wooden deck

1. String layout lines

2. Dig holes for post footings

3. Pour concrete for footings

4. Install posts

5. Add beams and joists

6. Install decking boards

7. Add stairs, if any

8. Install railings

9. Add fascia and other trim, as required

10. Seal or stain wood

SKILSAW

MAG 77

CIRCULAR SAW

HAND SET

MASON'S HAMMER

BRICK SET

WATER LEVEL

Design
and Photography Credits

DESIGN

Front Matter and Credits

1 Architect: Josh Chandler; Garden design: Susan Getz **3** Architect: Terry Martin; Landscape designer: Irving Tamura **5** Marilyn and Terry Boyd **127** Ron Mann

Ideas and Inspiration

6 Design: Robert Glazier, Hill Glazier Architects; Landscape design: Andrew Glazier, Wild West Gardens **7 left** Bob Swain **7 right** Landscape architect: John Montgomery, ASLA, Garden Architecture (www.garden-architecture.com) **8 top** Courtesy of Fireclay Tile **8 bottom** David Gibson, The Garden Collection **9** Heuttl-Thuilot Associates **10 top right** Jeff Zischke **10 bottom** Nancy and Greg Putnam, Putnam Construction **11 top left** Bob Clark **11 top right** Landscape architect: Sam Williamson **11 bottom** Landscape architect: John Montgomery, ASLA, Garden Architecture (www.garden-architecture.com) **12** Flower to the People **13 top** Clemens & Associates **13 bottom** Roger Fiske and Margo Partridge **14 top left** Jeffrey Bale **15 top right** Yunghi Choi **15 bottom right** Mathew Henning **16 top** Artist: Keeyla Meadows **16 bottom** Landscape architect: John Montgomery, ASLA, Garden Architecture (www.garden-architecture.com); Tile design: Kathleen Roney **17** Architect: Brion S. Jeanette & Associates, Inc. **18** Koch Landscape Architecture (www.kochla.com) **19 top** Topher Delaney **19 bottom** Kane Design and Associates **20 bottom** Designer/builder: Steven Rodriguez **21** Élan Landscape Design & Build **22 top** Landscape architect: John Montgomery, ASLA, Garden Architecture (www.garden-architecture.com) **22 bottom** Robert Trachtenberg/Garden Architecture **23** Architect: Churchill & Hambelton Architects **24** Design: Gary Marsh Design (www.garymarshdesign.com); Builder: John Perry Construction **25 top** Landscape architect: James Bradanini, Bradanini & Associates **25 bottom** Design: Gary Marsh Design (www.garymarshdesign.com); Builder: John Perry Construction **26** Landscape architect: Williamson Landscape Architects; Architect: Snyder Hartung + Kane; Construction: John Brown Builder **27 left** Mark Laurence **27 top right** Design: Gary Marsh Design (www.garymarshdesign.com); Contractor: Steve Rempe **27 bottom right** Landscape architects: Tom Berger and David Guthrie **28 left** Design: Gary Marsh Design (www.garymarshdesign.com); Builder: All Decked Out® Maureen Busby **28 right** Maureen Busby **29 middle left** Carol and Jim Stewart **29 bottom left** David Helm **29 top right** Design: Gary Marsh Design (www.garymarshdesign.com); Builder: All Decked Out® **30 bottom** John Harlow Jr., Harlow Gardens **31** David Rivera, Nahemow Rivera Group (www.nahemowriveragroup.com) **32** Landscape architect: John Montgomery, ASLA, Garden Architecture (www.garden-architecture.com) **33 top** Jeffrey Trent, Natural Order, and Ed Kisto **33 bottom** Linda Applewhite & Associates **34** Larry Feeney **35** Jeff Zischke **36** Claudia Schmutzler and Jeanie Werner **37 top left** Katelman Associates **37 top right** Architect: Carol A. Wilson **37 bottom** John Kenyon, Sundance Landscaping **38 bottom** Jay Ferguson **39** Van-Martin Rowe Design of Pasadena **40 top** Landscape architect: Lankford Associates **41 top** Marni Leis Design **41 bottom** Anne-Marie and Jeff Allen, Allen Landscaping **42** Architect: John Hermannson; Design and installation: Toni Deser and Paul Rodman **43 top** Architects: Manuela King, Bradanini & Associates, and Endres Ware, Architects **43 bottom** Oehme, van Sweden & Associates **44 bottom** Richard Faylor **45** Artistic Botanical Creations **46 top** Sonny Garcia and Tom Valva **46 bottom** Michael Glassman and Associates **47 top** Bernard Trainor Design Associates **47 bottom** Barbara Thompson **48 top** Theresa Clark, Landscape Architect **48 bottom** Garden design: Carrie Nimmer; Pool design: La Paz Pools **49** Landscape architect: R. M. Bradshaw & Associates **50 bottom** Wilson Associates **51** Design: Pamela Dreyfuss Interior Design; Exteriors Landscape Architecture **52** Landscape architect: The Berger Partnership; Pizza oven: Authentic Stone & Brickwork **53** Hardscape: Southwinds Landscaping & Pools; Softscape: Roger's Gardens **54 top** Greg Trutza/NewDirections in Landscape Architecture **54 bottom** Architect: Sam Wells & Associates; Stylist: Julie Atwood **55** Landscape architect: John Montgomery, ASLA, Garden Architecture (www.garden-architecture.com) **57** Greg Asbagh **58** Jean-Claude Hurni and Milan Havlin **59 top** Landscape architect: John Montgomery, ASLA, Garden Architecure (www.garden-architecture.com) **59 bottom** Greg Trutza **60** Landscape design: Kathleen Schaeffer, Great Gardens **61 top right** Garden designer: Thomas Hobbs **61 bottom right** John Showers **62 bottom** Robert and Judith Stitzel **63** Mike Snyder **64 top right** Ken Gordon England **65** Ron Lutsko, Lutsko Associates, and Freeland and Sabrina Tanner, Proscape Landscape Design **66** Diana Stratton, Diana Stratton Design **67 left** Greg Corman, Gardening Insights **67 bottom right** Tom Wilhite **69** Architect: Backen, Arragoni & Ross **70 bottom** Lighting design & installation: Berghoff Design Group; Technical support: Jonathan Hille **71 bottom** Topher Delaney **72 top right** Courtesy of Smith & Hawken **72 bottom** Gavin Landscaping **73 top** Jeff Zischke **73 bottom** Lighting by Garden & Security Lighting **74 bottom** Painter: John Simpson, The "Sky" Garden, designed by Fiona Lowrenson **75** Peter O. Whiteley **76** Design: Gary Marsh Design (www.garymarshdesign.com); Builder: All Decked Out® **77 left** Architect: Josh Chandler; Garden design: Susan Getz **77 bottom right** Jeffrey B. Glander & Associates **79 top** Dan Overbeck **79 bottom left** Landscape architect: John Montgomery, ASLA, Garden Architecture (www.garden-architecture.com) **79 bottom right** Peter O. Whiteley

A Shopper's Guide

How To Do It

PHOTOGRAPHY

Index